God's Call

God's Call

CHARLES FINNEY

Whitaker House

GOD'S CALL

ISBN: 0-88368-582-5
Printed in the United States of America
Copyright © 1999 by Whitaker House

Whitaker House
30 Hunt Valley Circle
New Kensington, PA 15068

Library of Congress Cataloging-in-Publication Data

Finney, Charles Grandison, 1792–1875.
    God's call / by Charles Finney.
       p.   cm.
    Sermons delivered at Oberlin College, 1845–1861.
    Contents: God's love for a sinful world — The excuses of sinners condemn God — The sinner's excuses answered — On refuges of lies — The wicked heart set to do evil — Moral insanity — Conditions of being saved — The sinner's natural power and moral weakness — Men often look highly upon what God abhors — Death to sin through Christ.
    ISBN: 0-88368-582-5
    1. Christian life Sermons. 2. Sin Sermons. 3. Sermons, American. 4. Congregational churches Sermons. I. Title.
BV4501.2.F484   1999
252'.058—dc21   99-39369

1 2 3 4 5 6 7 8 9 10 11 12 13 / 07 06 05 04 03 02 01 00 99

Contents

Preface

The following sermons are only a few of the many preached by Charles Finney at Oberlin College during the years 1845–1861. Few preachers in any age have surpassed Finney in clear and well-defined views of conscience and of man's moral convictions. Few have been more fully at home in the domain of God's law and government. Few have learned more of the spiritual life from experience and from observation. Few have discerned the true from the false more closely, or have been more skillful in speaking forth their points clearly. Hence, these sermons anointed by God were full of spiritual power. They are given to the public in this form, in the hope that at least a measure of the same saving power may bless the reader.

One

God's Love for a Sinful World

For God so loved the world that He gave His only
begotten Son, that whoever believes in Him should not
perish but have everlasting life.
—John 3:16

S in is the most expensive thing in the universe;
nothing else costs as much as sin. Whether sin
is pardoned or unpardoned, its cost is infinitely
great. When sin is pardoned, its cost falls chiefly on
the great atoning Substitute, Jesus Christ; when
unpardoned, it falls on the head of the guilty sinner.

The existence of sin is a fact experienced everywhere, observed everywhere. With increasing hei-
nousness, sin abounds in the human race.

Sin is the violation of an infinitely important
law—God's law, which was designed to secure the
highest good of the universe. Obedience to this law is
essential to the good of all creation. Without obedience, there could be no blessedness even in heaven.

Because sin is a violation of this important law, it
cannot be treated lightly. No government can afford
to treat disobedience as something trivial, because
everything—the entire welfare of the government and
of all the governed—depends on obedience. The need
to guard this law and to punish disobedience is equal
to the value of the interests at stake.

The law of God cannot be dishonored by anything He does. However, it has been dishonored by the disobedience of man; thus, God stands by it even more in order to maintain its honor. The greatest dishonor is done to God's law by disowning, disobeying, and despising it, and sinful man has done all these things. Hence, because this law is not only good but also intrinsically necessary to the happiness of the governed, it becomes necessary, above all else, for the Lawgiver to vindicate His law.

Hence, sin has involved God's government in a matter of great expense. Either the law must be carried out at the expense of the well-being of the whole human race, or God must submit and suffer the worst results of disrespect to His law.

Take, for example, any human government. Suppose the righteous and necessary laws that it imposes are disowned and dishonored. In such a case, the violated law must be honored by carrying out its penalty. Otherwise, something else—probably something worse—must be endured. Transgression must be paid for by the loss of happiness, somewhere, and in vast amount.

In the case of God's government, it has been deemed advisable to provide a substitute—one who would save the sinner while still honoring the law. Once this was settled, the next great question was, *How will this expense be paid?*

Covering the Cost of Sin

The Bible informs us how this question was in fact answered. A voluntary offering was taken up. But who wanted to be the first to pledge a contribution?

Who wished to begin where so much was to be raised? Who was willing to make the first sacrifice? Who was willing take the first step in a project so vast? The Bible tells us. It began with the Infinite Father. He made the first great donation. He gave His only begotten Son. Then, having given His Son first, He freely gives all else that the situation can require.

First, He gave His Son to make the atonement for the violated law; then He gave His Holy Spirit to take charge of this work. The Son agreed to stand as the Representative of sinners, so that He might honor the law by suffering in their place. He poured out His blood; He freely offered His whole life of suffering upon the altar; He did not hide His face from those who spat on Him, nor His back from the lashes they gave Him; and He did not shrink from the harshest words that wicked men could heap on Him. Similarly, the Holy Spirit also unceasingly devotes Himself to self-denying efforts, in order to accomplish the great purpose.

If God had wanted an easier method, He could have turned against wicked men and sent them all down to hell, as He did when certain angels *"did not keep their proper domain"* (Jude 6). Rebellion broke out in heaven, and God did not tolerate it for long around His lofty throne. But in the case of man, God changed His course. He did not send them all to hell, but, to gain men's souls back to obedience and heaven, He devised a plan consisting of amazing self-denial and self-sacrifice.

Atonement for All Mankind

For whom was this great donation made? Our text verse says that *"God so loved the world,"*

11

meaning the whole race of men—not only a particular part, but the whole race. We know that the Atonement must have been made for the whole world; we know this not only from the Bible, but also from the nature of the case. Clearly, if the Atonement had not been made for the entire human race, no individual could ever know that it was made for himself; therefore, no one could believe in Christ and receive by faith the blessings of the Atonement. With such utter uncertainty as to who is included in these limited provisions, the whole donation would fail because no rational faith could accept it.

Suppose a will is made by a rich man bequeathing some property to certain unknown individuals described only as "the elect." They are not described other than by this term. Although the maker of the will knew the individuals in his mind, he left no description of them that anyone—neither the elect themselves, the courts, or any living mortal—could understand. Such a will is altogether null and void; no living man can claim anything under it. Even if the elect were described as residents of a particular town, no one would be any better for it. Since the will does not embrace all the residents of that town, nor does it define which residents, all is still lost. No one can make a definite claim.

Now, if the Atonement were made in this way, no living person would have any valid reason for believing himself to be one of the elect before receiving the message of the Gospel. Thus he would have no authority to believe and receive its blessings by faith. In fact, on this supposition, the Atonement would be entirely void—unless a special revelation is made to the persons for whom it is intended.

As the case is, however, the very fact that a man belongs to the race of Adam—the fact that he is human, born of woman—is all-sufficient. It brings him into the domain of Christ's sacrifice. He is one of the *"world"* for whom God gave His Son, *"that whoever believes in Him should not perish but have everlasting life."*

Love as God's Motive

God's motive for this great gift was love—love for the world. *"God so loved the world that He gave His...Son"* to die for it. God also loved the universe, but this gift of His Son sprang from love for our world. However, in this great act, He also took pains to provide for the interests of the universe. He was careful to do nothing that could in the least relax the sacredness of His law. He carefully intended to guard against any misunderstanding of His regard for His law and for the high interests of obedience and happiness in His moral universe. He meant to rule out, once and for all, the danger that any moral agent could be tempted to undervalue the moral law.

Furthermore, it was not only out of His love for souls, but also out of respect for the spirit of the law of His own eternal reason, that He gave up His Son to die. The plan to give up His Son originated in this: the law of His own reason would be honored and held sacred. God can do nothing inconsistent with its spirit. He must do everything possible to prevent the commission of sin and to secure the confidence and love of His subjects. These things were so sacred to Him that He would baptize His Son in His own blood sooner than endanger the good of the universe.

Beyond question, it was love and regard for the highest good of the universe that led Him to sacrifice His own beloved Son.

The Nature of God's Love

Let us consider more carefully the nature of this love. John 3:16 places special stress on this love— *"God so loved"* (emphasis added). His love was so wonderful and so unique in its character that it led Him to give up His only Son to die. More is evidently implied in this expression than simply its greatness. Unless we understand this point, we will be in danger of falling into the strange mistake of the Universalists,* who are always talking about God's love for sinners, but whose ideas of the nature of this love never lead to repentance or to holiness. They seem to think of this love as simply good nature, and they picture God only as a very good-natured being, whom nobody needs to fear. Such ideas do not incline one toward holiness, but in fact the very opposite. Only when we come to understand the true nature of this love can we feel its moral power promoting holiness.

One may reasonably ask, "If God so loved the world with a love characterized by greatness, and by greatness alone, why did He not save the whole world without sacrificing His Son?" This question shows us that there is deep meaning in the word *so*. Therefore, let us make a careful study of the love God has for the world.

---

* Universalism teaches that eventually everyone will be saved. Universalism began in the eighteenth century and later united with Unitarianism.

A Love Not Delighting in Man's Character

First, this love is not satisfaction with or a delight in the character of the human race. This could not be possible, for there was nothing pleasing in their character. For God to have loved such a race in this way would have been infinitely disgraceful to Himself.

A Paternal Love

Second, His love was not mere emotion or feeling. It was not a blind impulse, though many seem to suppose it was. It is often supposed that God acted as men do when they are carried away by strong emotion. But there could be no virtue in this. A man might give away all he is worth under such a blind impulse of feeling, but be none the more virtuous. Even so, we cannot exclude all emotion from God's love for a lost world. He had emotion, but not *only* emotion. Indeed, the Bible teaches us that God's love for man, lost in his sins, was paternal, like the love of a father for his children. In this case, God's love was for rebellious, disobedient, prodigal children. Of course, this love contains the deepest compassion.

A Fraternal Love

The third aspect of this love is that it was fraternal on the part of Christ. *"He is not ashamed to call them brethren"* (Heb. 2:11). On the one hand, Christ is acting for His siblings; on the other, for His children. The Father gave Him up for this work and of course shares in the love appropriate to the relationship.

A Love Not for God's Own Profit

Fourth, this love was altogether *disinterested*, which is to say that God had nothing to gain for

15

Himself by saving His children. Indeed, it is impossible to imagine God as being selfish, since His love embraces all creatures and all interests according to their real value. There is no doubt He took delight in saving the human race—why should He not? It is a great salvation in every sense. It increases the bliss of heaven, and it will greatly affect the glory and blessedness of the Infinite God. He will eternally respect Himself for having a love so unmotivated by personal gain. God knows that all His holy creatures will eternally respect Him for this work and for the love that gave it birth. But let it also be said that He knew they would not respect Him for this great work unless they could see that He did it for the good of sinners.

A Zealous Love

Fifth, this love was zealous, not the coldhearted state of mind that some people suppose it was. It was not a mere concept, but a deep, zealous, earnest love, burning in His soul like a fire that nothing can quench.

A Costly Love

Sixth, the sacrifice was a most self-denying one. Did it cost the Father nothing to give up His own beloved Son to suffer and die such a death? If this is not self-denial, what is? To give up His Son to so much suffering—is this not the noblest self-denial? The universe could never imagine great self-denial without His example.

A Particular yet Universal Love

Seventh, this love was particular because it was universal, and also universal because it was particular. God loved each sinner in particular; therefore, He loved all. Because He loved all impartially, with *"no respect of persons"* (Rom. 2:11 KJV), He therefore loved each in particular.

A Patient Love

Eighth, this was a most patient love. It is rare to find a parent who so loves his child that he is never impatient. How many of you parents can say that you love all your children so well that you have never felt impatient toward any of them? Can you take them in your arms when they are being disobedient and love them out of their sins, love them into repentance? Of which of your children can you say, "Thank God, I never became impatient with that child"? And if you were to meet him in heaven, could you say, "I never caused that child to become impatient with me"? Often have I heard parents say, "I love my children, but oh, how my patience fails me!" And, after the dear ones are dead, you may hear their bitter moans, "Oh, how could I have caused my child so much stumbling and so much sin?"

But God is never impatient. His love is so deep and so great that He is always patient.

Sometimes, when parents have children who are unfortunate in some way, they can bear with anything from them. But when the children are very wicked, parents seem to feel that their impatience is quite excusable. In God's case, the children are not unfortunate, but intensely wicked—knowingly wicked. But oh, His amazing patience! He is so set upon their good, so desirous of their highest welfare, that however they abuse Him, He sets Himself to bless them still, and to melt them into penitence and love, by the death of His Son in their place!

A Jealous Love

Ninth, this is a jealous love, not in a bad sense, but in a good sense. This love is jealous in the sense of being exceedingly careful that nothing will occur to injure those He loves. Similarly, a husband and wife who truly love each other are jealous with ever wakeful jealousy over each other's welfare, seeking always to do all they can to promote each other's true interests.

Salvation for All Who Believe

This donation of God's Son has already been made—not only promised, but actually made. The promise, given long before, has been fulfilled. The Son has come, has died, has made the ransom, and lives to offer eternal life. This salvation is prepared for all who will embrace it.

The Son of God did not die to appease vengeance, as some seem to understand the matter, but He died under the demands of law. The law had been violated and thereby dishonored. Therefore, Christ accepted the responsibility of honoring it by fulfilling its demands through His suffering life and His atoning death. He did not die to appease a vindictive spirit in God, but to secure the highest good of the universe in a dispensation of mercy.

Since this atonement has been made, all mankind has a right to it. It is open to everyone who will embrace it. Though Jesus remains the Father's Son, by gracious right He belongs in an important sense to the human race—to everyone; every sinner has a share in His blood if he will only come humbly forward and claim it. God sent His Son to be the Savior of the world—of anyone who would believe and accept this great salvation.

God gives His Spirit in order to apply this salvation to men. He comes to each man's door and knocks, to gain admittance, if He can, and to show each sinner that he may now have salvation. Oh, what a labor of love this is!

This salvation must be received by faith, if it is to be received at all. This is the only possible way. God's government over sinners is moral, not physical, because the sinner is himself a moral and not a physical agent. Therefore, God cannot influence us in any way unless we will give Him our confidence. He can never save us by merely taking us away to some place called heaven—as if a change of place would change the human heart. Therefore, there can be no possible way to be saved except by simple faith.

A Living and Reigning Christ

Now, do not suppose that embracing the Gospel is simply to believe these historical facts without truly receiving Christ as your Savior. If this had been the plan, then Christ needed only to come down and die, then go back to heaven and quietly wait to see who would believe the facts. But how different is the real case! Christ comes down to fill the soul with His own life and love. Repentant sinners hear and believe the truth concerning Jesus, and then receive Christ into the soul, so that He may live there and reign supreme forever.

Many people misunderstand this point, saying, "If I believe the facts as matters of history, it is enough." No! No! This is not it by any means. *"With the heart one believes unto righteousness"* (Rom. 10:10). The Atonement was made to provide the way so that Jesus could come down to human hearts and draw them into union and harmony with Himself; so that God could embrace sinners in the arms of His love; so that law and government would not be dishonored even though God manifested friendship toward sinners. But the Atonement will by no means save sinners just by its having prepared the way for them to come into harmony and fellowship of heart with God.

Now Jesus comes to each sinner's door and knocks (Rev. 3:20). Listen! What's that knocking? Why did Jesus not go away and stay in heaven, until men would simply believe the historical facts and be baptized, as some suppose, for salvation? But now, see how He comes down, tells the sinner what He has done, reveals all His love, tells him how holy and sacred it is—so sacred that He cannot act without reference to the holiness of His law and the purity of His government. Thus impressing on the heart the deepest ideas of His holiness and purity, He enforces the need for true repentance and the sacred duty of renouncing all sin.

REMARKS

1. The Bible teaches that sinners may forfeit their birthright and put themselves beyond the

reach of mercy. I said earlier that it is necessary that God guard Himself against the abuses of His love. Because circumstances can create the greatest danger of such abuse, He must make sinners know that they may not abuse His love without punishment.

2. Under the Gospel, sinners are under the greatest possible responsibility. They are in the utmost danger of trampling down beneath their feet the very Son of God (Heb. 10:29). *"Come,"* they say, *"let us kill him, and the inheritance will be ours"* (Mark 12:7). When God sends forth, last of all, His own beloved Son, what do they do? They add to all their other sins and rebellions the highest insult to this glorious Son! Suppose something analogous to this were done under a human government. A case of rebellion occurs in some of the provinces. The king sends his own son—not with an army to cut them down quickly in their rebellion—but the son goes among them gently, meekly, and patiently, explaining the laws of the kingdom and exhorting them to obedience. What do they do in the case? With one consent they combine to seize him and put him to death!

But perhaps you disagree with the application of this truth and ask me, "Who murdered the Son of God? Were they not Jews?" Yes, but have you, sinners, had no part in this murder? Has not your treatment of Jesus Christ shown that you are most fully in agreement with the ancient Jews in their murder of the Son of God? If you had been there, would anyone have shouted louder than you, *"Away with Him, away with Him! Crucify Him!"* (John 19:15)? Have you not always said, *"Depart from us, for we do not desire the knowledge of Your ways"* (Job 21:14)?

3. It was said of Christ, *"Though He was rich…
He became poor, that you through His poverty might
become rich"* (2 Cor. 8:9). How strikingly true this is!
Our redemption cost Christ His life; it found Him
rich but made Him poor; it found us infinitely poor
but made us rich, even to all the wealth of heaven.
But no one can partake of these riches until he ac-
cepts them for himself in the legitimate way. They
must be received on the terms proposed, or else the
offer passes utterly away, and you are left poorer
than if no such treasures had ever been laid at your
feet.

Many people seem to misunderstand this case
entirely. They seem not to believe what God says,
but keep saying *if*—"If only there were any salvation
for me, if only there were an atonement provided for
the pardon of my sins." This was one of the last
things that was cleared up in my mind before I fully
committed my soul to trust God. I had been studying
the Atonement. I saw what it demanded of the sinner, but it irritated me, and I said, "If I should become a Christian, how could I know what God would
do with me?" Because I was thus irritated, I said
foolish and bitter things against Christ—until my
soul was horrified at its own wickedness, and I said,
"I will make things right with Christ if it is possible
to do so."

In this way, many people come to the Gospel as
if it were only a chance, an experiment. They take
each forward step most carefully, with fear and
trembling, as if there were the utmost doubt
whether there could be any mercy for them. It was
the same with me. I was on my way to my office,
when the question came before my mind: "What are

you waiting for? You need not make it so difficult; everything is already done. You have only to agree to the proposition—give your heart right up to it at once—this is all." And so it is.

All Christians and sinners ought to understand that the whole plan is complete, that the whole of Christ—His character, His work, His atoning death, and His ever living intercession—belongs to each and every man, and needs only to be accepted. There is a full ocean of salvation. *There it is.* You may take it just as easily as you may pass it by. It is as if you stood on the shore of an ocean of soft, pure water, dying with thirst. You are welcome to drink, and you need not have any fear of exhausting that ocean or of depriving anyone else by drinking from it yourself. You need not feel that the ocean of waters is not free to you; you are invited and encouraged to drink— yes, to drink abundantly!

This ocean supplies all your need. You do not need to have the attributes of Jesus Christ in yourself, for His attributes become yours for all possible use. As the Scripture says, He *"became for us wisdom from God; and righteousness and sanctification and redemption"* (1 Cor. 1:30). What do you need? Wisdom? Here it is. Righteousness? Here it is. Sanctification? Here you have it. All is in Christ. Can you possibly think of any one thing necessary for your moral purity or your usefulness that is not here in Christ? Nothing. All is provided here. Therefore, you need not say, "I will go and pray and try." There is no need to sing,

> I'll go to Jesus tho' my sin
> Hath like a mountain rose,

> *Perhaps* He will admit my plea;
> *Perhaps* will hear my prayer.

There is no need for any *perhaps* here. The doors are always open—like the doors of Broadway Tabernacle in New York, made to swing open and hold themselves open, so that they could not swing back and shut upon the crowds of people passing through.

So the door of salvation is always open—fastened open, and no man can shut it—not the Pope, or the Devil, or any angel from heaven or from hell. There it stands, all swung back, and the passage is wide open for every sinner of the human race to enter if he is willing.

4. Again I will say that sin is the most expensive thing in the universe. Are you well aware, sinner, what a price has been paid for you so that you may be redeemed and be made an heir of God and of heaven? Oh, what an expensive business for you to indulge in sin!

And what an enormous tax the government of God has paid to redeem this province from its ruin! All the taxes in the world are nothing compared with the sin tax of Jehovah's government—that awful sin tax! Think how much machinery is kept in motion to save sinners! The Son of God was sent down; angels are sent as *"ministering spirits"* to the heirs of salvation (Heb. 1:14); missionaries are sent; Christians labor, pray, and weep in deep and anxious concern—all to seek and save the lost.

What an enormous tax is levied upon the benevolence of the universe in order to put away sin and to save the sinner! If the cost could be computed in solid gold, what a world it would be—a solid globe of gold in itself! What an array of toil and expense from angels, Jesus Christ, the Divine Spirit, and living men! Shame on sinners who hold on to sin despite all these benevolent efforts to save them! Instead of being ashamed out of their sin, they will say, "Let God pay this tax; who cares! Let the missionaries labor, let pious women work their very fingers off to raise funds to keep all this human machinery in motion; what is all this to me? I have loved my pleasures, and I will run after them!" What an unfeeling heart this is!

It costs a great deal to rid society of certain forms of sin, as for example, slavery. Much has been expended to rid our land of this sore evil. So many lives and so much agony to get rid of this one sin!

Woe to those who attempt to capitalize on the sins of men! Just think of the bartender—tempting men while God is trying to dissuade them from rushing on in the ways of sin and death! Think of the guilt of those who thus position themselves to fight against God! So Christ has to contend with bartenders and others who are doing all they can to hinder His work.

5. Sinners can very well afford to make sacrifices to save their fellow sinners. Paul could do so for his fellow sinners. He felt that he had done his part toward making sinners, and then he felt he must also do his part in converting them back to God. Suppose a young man thinks he cannot afford to be a minister, for he is afraid he will not be well supported. But does he not owe something to the grace that saved his soul from hell? Has he not some sacrifices to make, since Jesus has made so many for him? And

Christians, too, who were in Christ before him—did they not pray and suffer and toil for his soul's salvation? As to his danger of lacking bread in the Lord's work, let him trust his great Master.

Let me also say that churches may be greatly at fault for not comfortably supporting their pastors. God will surely starve them if they starve their ministers. Their own souls and the souls of their children will be barren as death if they greedily starve those whom God in His providence sends to feed them with the Bread of Life.

6. This subject strikingly illustrates the nature of sin as mere selfishness. The sinner does not care how much sin costs Jesus Christ—how much it costs the church, how much it taxes the benevolent sympathies and the self-sacrificing labors of all the good in earth or heaven. These things do not matter to the sinner; he loves self-indulgence and will have it while he can. How many of you have cost your friends countless tears and trouble to get you back from your ways of sin? Are you not ashamed, when so much has been done for you, that you cannot be persuaded to give up your sins and turn to God and holiness?

God's whole effort toward man is one of suffering and self-denial. Beginning with the sacrifice of His own beloved Son, it is carried on with ever renewed sacrifices and toilsome labors—all at great expense. Just think how much time these efforts have taken already. Think of how many tears, poured out like water, they have cost. Think of how much pain in many forms this enterprise has caused and cost. Indeed, the very sin that you roll as a sweet morsel under your tongue—God will certainly hate it when He sees how much it costs, and He will say, *"Oh, do not do this abominable thing that I hate!"* (Jer. 44:4).

Yet God is not unhappy in these self-denials. So great is His joy in the results, that He deems all the suffering as something trivial in comparison, even as earthly parents enjoy the efforts they make to bless their children. Though their toil is great, they love their children so intensely that their joy is also great.

Such is the labor, the joy, and the self-denial of the Father, the Son, and the Holy Spirit in their great work for human salvation. Often they are grieved that so many refuse to be saved. As they toil with a common purpose, there is nothing, within reasonable limits, that they will not do or suffer to accomplish their great work. It is wonderful to think how all creation sympathizes, too, in this work and its necessary sufferings. Go back to the scene of Christ's sufferings. Could the sun in the heavens look down unmoved on such a scene? No, the sun turned its back and could not look down on such a spectacle! (See Luke 23:45.) All nature seemed to put on its robes of deepest mourning. The scene was too much for even inanimate nature to bear.

7. This subject also forcibly illustrates the worth of the soul. Do you think God would have done all this if He had had the low views on this subject that sinners usually have? The results will fully justify all the expense. God had well counted the cost before He began. Long before He formed a moral universe, He knew perfectly what it would cost Him to redeem sinners, and He knew that the result would amply justify all the cost. He knew that a wonder of mercy

would be worked; that the suffering demanded of Christ, great as it was, would be endured; and that results infinitely glorious would accrue from there.

God looked down the track of time into the distant ages—where, as the cycles roll along, one might see the joys of redeemed saints who are singing their songs and striking their harps anew with the everlasting song through the long eternity of their blessedness. Was this not enough for the heart of Infinite Love to enjoy? What do you think of it, Christian? Will you not say now, "I am ashamed to ask to be forgiven. How can I bear to receive such mercy? It is the price of blood; how can I accept it? How can I place upon Jesus so much expense?"

You are right in saying that you have cost Him great expense, but the expense has been cheerfully met. The pain has all been endured and will not need to be endured again, and it will cost no more if you accept than if you decline. Moreover, let it be considered that Jesus Christ has not acted unwisely; He did not pay too much for the soul's redemption—not a pang more than the interests of God's government demanded and the worth of the soul would justify.

When you come to see Him face to face and tell Him what you think of it, will you not adore the wisdom that manages this plan, and the infinite love in which it had its birth? Oh, what will you then say of the amazing condescension that brought down Jesus to your rescue? Dear Christian, have you not often poured out your soul before your Savior in acknowledgment of what you have cost Him? Was there not a kind of lifting up, as if the very bottom of your soul were to rise, and you would pour out your whole heart? If anybody had seen you, he would have wondered what had happened to you that had so melted your soul in gratitude and love.

Now, sinners, will you sell your birthright? How much will you take for it? How much will you accept for your share in Christ? For how much will you sell your soul? But what an idea—to sell your Christ! At one time He was sold for thirty pieces of silver (see Matthew 26:15), and ever since, the heavens have been raining tears of blood on our guilty world. If you were to be asked by the Devil to set a sum for which you would sell your soul, what would be the price named?

Lorenzo Dow, a pioneer Methodist preacher, once met a man as he was riding along a road to fulfill an appointment. Dow said to the man, "Friend, have you ever prayed?" "No," was the answer. "How much money will you take never to pray?" "One dollar." And so Dow paid the dollar and rode on. The man put the money in his pocket and went on his way, thinking. The more he thought, the worse he felt. "There," he said, "I have sold my soul for one dollar! It must be that I have met the Devil! Nobody else would tempt me so. With all my soul I must repent, or be damned forever!"

How often have you bargained to sell your Savior for less than thirty pieces of silver—no, for even a dollar? Repent so that you will be saved.

8. Finally, God wants volunteers to help in this great work. God has given Himself, given His Son, and sent His Spirit, but more laborers still are needed. What will you give? Paul said, *"I bear in my body the marks of the Lord Jesus"* (Gal. 6:17). Do you aspire to such an honor? What will you do? What

will you suffer? Do not say, "I have nothing to give."
You can give yourself—your eyes, your ears, your
hands, your mind, your heart, your all. Surely
nothing you have is too sacred and too good to be
devoted to such a work, upon such a call! How many
young men are ready to go? How many young
women? Whose heart leaps up, crying, *"Here am I!
Send me"* (Isa. 6:8)?

Two

The Excuses of Sinners Condemn God

Would you indeed annul My judgment? Would you condemn Me that you may be justified?
—Job 40:8

E ven in his anguish while undergoing his sore trials, Job had generally spoken correctly of God. But he had said some things that were hasty and abusive. For these the Lord rebuked him. This rebuke is contained in the context of Job 40:

> *Moreover the LORD answered Job, and said: "Shall the one who contends with the Almighty correct Him? He who rebukes God, let him answer it." Then Job answered the LORD and said: "Behold, I am vile; what shall I answer You? I lay my hand over my mouth. Once I have spoken, but I will not answer; yes, twice, but I will proceed no further." Then the LORD answered Job out of the whirlwind, and said: "Now prepare yourself like a man; I will question you, and you shall answer Me: Would you indeed annul My judgment? Would you condemn Me that you may be justified?"*
>
> *(Job 40:1–8)*

It is not, however, my intention to discuss the original purpose of these words, but rather to consider how they may be applied to the case of sinners. In doing so, I will first show that every excuse for sin condemns God. We will then consider some of these excuses in detail and show that excuses for sin add insult to injury.

Every Excuse Condemns God

The fact that every excuse for sin condemns God is clear if we consider that nothing can be sin for which there is a justifiable excuse. Also, if God condemns the thing for which there is a good excuse, He must be wrong. This is self-evident. If God condemns what we have good reason for doing, no intelligent being in the universe can justify Him. But God does condemn all sin. He condemns it utterly and will not allow the least defense or excuse for it. Thus, either there is no defense for it, or God is wrong. Consequently, every excuse for sin places blame upon God and virtually accuses Him of tyranny. Whoever pleads an excuse for sin, therefore, charges God with blame.

What Are These Excuses?

Let us consider some of these excuses and see whether the principles I have laid down are not just and true.

Inability to Repent

No excuse is more common than the inability to repent. It is echoed and reechoed over every Christian land, handed down age after age, never to be forgotten. With no embarrassment whatsoever, it is proclaimed that men cannot do what God requires of them.

Let us examine this and see what it amounts to. It is said that God requires what men cannot do. If this is true, does God know that men cannot do it? Most certainly, for He knows all things. Then the requirement is most unreasonable. Human reason can never justify it. It is a natural impossibility.

But upon what penalty does God require men to do what they cannot do? The threatened penalty is eternal death! Yes, eternal death, according to the views of those who plead inability as an excuse. God requires me, on pain of eternal death, to do what He knows I cannot do. Truly this condemns God in the worst sense. You might just as well charge God outright with being an infinite tyrant. What is more, we cannot help charging God with infinite tyranny, because the law of our reason demands it.

Perhaps, sinner, when you use the excuse of inability, you do not think that you are really accusing God of infinite tyranny. And you, Christian, who make this dogma of inability a part of your "orthodox" creed, may not have noticed how it blasphemes the character of God; but your failure to notice it does not alter the fact. The charge against God is involved in the very doctrine of inability and cannot be explained out of it.

I have indicated that this charge is blasphemous against God, and surely it is. Will God require men to do the impossible and yet proclaim eternal death upon them for not doing what they have no natural power to do? Never! Far be it from God to do any

such thing! Yet both good and bad men accuse God
of doing this very thing, not once or twice, but
throughout all the ages, with all men, from the beginning to the end of time! Horrible! Nothing in all
the government of God ever so insulted and abused
Jehovah! Nothing was ever more blasphemous and
false! God's Word says that *"His commandments are
not burdensome"* (1 John 5:3), but you, by this excuse of inability, proclaim that God's words are false.
You declare that His commands are not only burdensome, but are even naturally impossible! Listen!
What does the Lord Jesus say? *"My yoke is easy and
My burden is light"* (Matt. 11:30). Do you deny
this? Do you rise up in the very face of His words
and say, "Lord, Your yoke is so hard that no man
can possibly endure it; Your burden is so heavy
that no man can ever bear it"? Is this not contra-
dicting and blaspheming Him who cannot lie? (See
Titus 1:2.)

But you insist that no man can obey the law of
God. The Presbyterian Confession of Faith says, "No
man is able, either by himself or by any grace received in this life, to keep the commandments of God
perfectly; but he daily breaks them in thought, word,
and deed." This affirms not only that no man is
naturally able to keep God's commands, but also
that no man is able to do it "by any grace received in
this life." This declaration is an attack on the Gospel
as well as a misrepresentation of the law of its
Author, and of man's relationship to both. If there is
a lie either in hell or out of hell, this declaration is a
lie, or else God is an infinite tyrant. If Reason were
allowed to speak at all, it would be impossible for her
to say less or otherwise. And has God not created the

mind of man for the very purpose of taking notice of the integrity of all His ways?

Let God be true, though every man be proved a liar (Rom. 3:4)! In the present case, the fact that no man can say that he is truly unable to keep the law, shows that man lies, not God.

Lack of Time

A second excuse that sinners make is lack of time. Suppose I tell one of my sons, "Go, do this or that duty, or else you will be whipped to death." He replies, "Father, I can't possibly do it, for I do not have time. I must be doing the other business that you told me to do. Besides, even if I had nothing else to do, I could not possibly do this new business in the time you allow." Now, if this statement were the truth, and I knew it when I gave him the command, then I am undeniably a tyrant. My conduct toward my son is downright tyranny.

So if God really requires of you what you do not have time to do, He is infinitely to blame. For He surely knows how little time you have, and it is undeniable that He enforces His requirements with most dreadful penalties. What! Is God so careless of justice? Is He so unmindful of the well-being of His creatures that He will amuse Himself by hurling red-hot bolts of lightning among His unfortunate creatures, despite what is just and right? Never! This is not true; it is only the false assumption that the sinner makes when he uses the excuse that he does not have time to do what God demands of him.

Let me ask you, sinner, how much time will it take you to do the first great duty that God requires, namely, to give Him your heart? How long will this

take? How long do you need in order to make up
your mind to serve and love God? Do you not know
that this, when it is done, is done in only a moment
of time? How much time do you need in order to persuade yourself to do it?

Your meaning may be this: "Lord, it takes me so
long to make up my mind to serve You, it seems as if I
will never get time enough for this. Life itself seems
almost too short for me to bring my mind to this un-
welcome decision." Is this your meaning, sinner?

Let us look at the subject from all sides. Suppose
I say to my son, "Do this now, my son," and he replies, "I can't, Father, for I must do that other thing
you told me to do." Does God do this? No. God only
requires the duty of each moment in its time. This is
all. He only asks us to use faithfully the power that
He has given us so far—nothing more. He only requires that we do the best we can. When He dictates
the amount of love that will please Him, He does not
say, "You shall love the Lord your God with the
powers of an angel." No, but He says, *"With all your
heart"* (Deut. 6:5)—this is all. This plea of the sinner—that he cannot love God with all his heart,
mind, and strength—is infinitely ridiculous. God
says to the sinner, "You shall do the best that you
are able to do." The sinner says, "But I am not able
to do that." Oh, what stupid nonsense!

You accuse God of being unreasonable. The
truth is, God is the most reasonable of all beings. He
asks only that we use each moment for Him, either
in labor or in rest, whichever is most for His glory.
He only requires that with the time, talents, and
strength that He has given us, we should do all we
can to serve Him.

A mother says, "How can I be religious? I have to take care of all my children." Indeed, you do have to take care of your children. But can't you find time to serve God? God does not require that you forsake and neglect your children, but He asks you to take good care of them and to do it all for Him. He says to you, "These are My children," as He puts them into your hands. "Take care of them for Me, and I will give you wages." It will not require more time to take care of your children for God than to take care of them for yourself. But you say, "I cannot be religious, for I must be up in the morning and get my breakfast." How much longer will it take you to please God while you get your breakfast ready than to do the same to please yourself? How much more time must you have to do your duties religiously than to do them selfishly?

What, then, do you mean by this plea? The fact is, all these excuses show that the excuser is infatuated with foolishness. Which of God's requirements is so great that you do not have enough time to do it? Only the requirement that you should do everything for God. People who make this plea seem to have entirely overlooked the real nature of religion and the requirements that God places on them. It is the same with the plea of inability. The sinner says, "I am unable." Unable to do what? Exactly what you are able to do, for God never requires anything beyond this. Therefore, unless you assume that God requires of you more than you can do, you are well aware that your plea is false, and even ridiculous. If, on the other hand, you do assume this, then your plea would still not show God to be unjust.

In this plea of having no time to be religious, men entirely overlook or misinterpret the true idea of religion. The farmer pleads, "I can't be religious; I can't serve God; I must sow my wheat." Well, sow your wheat, but do it for the Lord (1 Cor. 10:31). You may think you have so much to do. Then do it all for the Lord. A student says, "I can't be religious, for I must study my lesson." Well, study, but do so for the Lord, and this effort will be religious. The man who neglects to sow his wheat or to study his lessons because he wants to be religious is crazy. He perverts the plainest things in the worst way. If you are to be religious, you must also be industrious. The farmer must sow his wheat, and the student must study his lesson. An idle man can no more be religious than the Devil can be.

This idea that men can't be religious because they have something else to do is nonsense. It utterly overlooks the great truth that God never forbids us to do the appropriate business of life. He only requires that we do everything for Him. If God required us to serve Him in a way that would cause us to neglect the practical duties of life, it would truly be a hard case. But the truth is that He requires us to do precisely these duties and to do them all honestly and faithfully for Him in the best possible manner. Let the farmer take care of his farm, but let him see that he does it well and, above all, does it for God. It is God's farm, and the heart of every farmer is God's heart. Therefore, let the farm be tilled for God, and let the heart be devoted to Him alone.

A Sinful Nature

Men also plead their sinful nature as an excuse for their sin. What is this sinful nature? Does it mean that all your powers and abilities and even the very essence of your body were poisoned, were made sinful in Adam, and were passed on to you in this polluted state? Does it mean that you were so born in sin that the substance of your being is all saturated with it, and that all the powers of your body and mind are themselves *sin?* Do you believe this?

If this were true, it would indeed make for a difficult case. A difficult case indeed! Until the laws of my reason are changed, it would compel me to speak out openly and say, "Lord, this is a difficult case: You have made my nature sinful, and yet You charge the guilt of its sin upon me!" I could not help saying this; the deep echoings of my inner being would proclaim it without ceasing, and the breaking of ten thousand thunderbolts over my head would not deter me from thinking and saying so. My ability to reason, an ability that God has given me, would forever affirm it.

But this is utterly absurd, for what is sin? God answers, *"Sin is the transgression of the law"* (1 John 3:4 KJV). Yet you believe that your nature is itself a breach of the law of God, that it has always been a breach of God's law, from Adam to the day of your birth. You say that this sin was passed down in the veins and blood of the human race. And who made it so? Who created the veins and blood of man? From whose hand sprang this physical body and this mind? Was man his own creator? Did sin play a part in the work of creating your physical makeup? Can one believe such a thing? No, your nature and its original faculties were created by God; therefore, you are accusing Him of the guilty authorship of your sinful nature.

How strange this is! If man is at fault for his sinful nature, why not also condemn him for having blue or brown eyes? The fact is, sin does not occur because we have a nature or because of the qualities of that nature, but only because of the bad use we make of our nature. This is all. Our Maker will never find fault with us for what He has Himself done or made. He will not condemn us, if we will only make a right use of our powers—of our minds, our emotions, and our wills. He never holds us responsible for our original nature. You will find that God has given no law dictating what sort of nature and physical powers we should have. If He had given a law on these points, we might see the transgression of them as the definition of sin. But since there is no law about nature, nature cannot be a transgression.

Here let me say that, if God were to make a law dictating what nature or physical makeup a man must have, it could not possibly be anything but unjust and absurd. This is because man's nature is not subject to legislation, precept, and penalty; it lies entirely outside the domain of voluntary action, or of any action of man at all. And yet thousands of men have held the belief that sin consists in great part in having a sinful nature. Yes, throughout history, theologians have taught this monstrous dogma. It has resounded from pulpits and has been repeated over and over. Moreover, men have never seemed to grow weary of glorifying this dogma as the surest test of sound orthodoxy. Orthodoxy! There never was a more infamous libel against Jehovah! It would be hard to name another dogma that more violently outrages common sense. It is nonsense—absurd and utter nonsense! Think what harm it has done! Think how it has scandalized the law, the government, and the character of God! Think how it has filled the mouths of sinners with excuses from the day of its birth to this hour!

Now, I do not mean to imply that the men who have held this dogma have knowingly insulted God with it. I do not imply that they have been aware of the impious and even blasphemous bearings of this dogma upon Jehovah. I am happy to think that at least some people have done all this mischief ignorantly. But the harm has not been lessened because of the honest ignorance in which it has been done.

A Great Difficulty

Sinners, in excusing their sin, say they are willing to be Christians. They say they are willing to be sanctified. Oh, yes, they are very willing, but there is some great difficulty or something else. Perhaps they do not know just what or where it is, but it is somewhere, and it will not let them become Christians.

Now, the fact is, if we are really willing, there is nothing more that we can do. To be willing is all we have to do *morally* in the case, and all we can do. But the plea in the sinner's mouth insists that God requires of us what is naturally impossible. It assumes that God requires of us something more than to be willing; and this, to us, is of course an impossibility. If I will to move my muscles and no motion follows, I have done all I can do; there is a difficulty beyond my reach, and I am not to blame for its existence or for its hindrance. Similarly, if I will to serve God and absolutely no effect follows, then I have done my utmost, and God cannot demand anything more. In

41

fact, to will is the very thing that God does require. *"For if there is first a willing mind, it is accepted"* (2 Cor. 8:12). Dear parent, if you had told your child to do anything, and you saw him exerting himself to the utmost, would you ask for anything more? If you were to see a parent demanding of a child more than he could possibly do, however willing the child may be, would you not denounce that parent as a tyrant? Certainly you would. Even a slave driver is not likely to beat his slave if he sees him willing to do all he can.

This plea that there is some great difficulty beyond willingness is utterly false, for no sinner is willing to be any better than he actually is. If the will is right, all is right. Therefore, those who plead that they are willing to be Christians while they remain in their sins talk mere nonsense.

Awaiting God's Time

Sinners say they are waiting for God's time. A lady in Philadelphia had been in great distress of mind for many years. When I went to see her, I asked, "What does God require of you? What is your case?" "Oh," she said, "God waited on me a long time before I began to seek Him at all, and now I must wait for Him as long as He did for me. So my minister tells me. You see, therefore, that I am waiting in great distress for God to receive me."

Now, what is the real meaning of this? This woman was essentially saying, "God tells me to come to the Gospel feast, and I am ready, but He is not ready to let me in." Does this not throw all the blame upon God, more than anything else possibly could? The sinner says, "I am ready, willing, and waiting; but God is not yet ready for me to stop sinning. His hour has not yet come."

When I first began to preach, I found this idea to be almost universal. After pressing men to their duty of accepting the Gospel, I would often be accosted by men and women saying, "What? You throw all the blame upon the sinner!" "Yes, indeed I do," would be my reply. An old lady once met me after a sermon and began to cry out, "You tell men to get religion themselves! You tell them to repent themselves! You don't mean this, do you?" "Indeed, I do," I said. She had been teaching for many years that the sinner's chief duty is to await God's time.

Special Circumstances

Another excuse of sinners is that their circumstances are unusual. They say, "I know my duty well enough, but my circumstances are so unique." But does God not understand your circumstances? Has His providence not been concerned in making them what they are? If so, then you are throwing blame upon God. You say, "O Lord, You are a hard master, for You never made any allowance for my circumstances."

But how much, sinner, do you really mean in making this plea? Do you mean that your circumstances are so abnormal that God ought to excuse you from becoming religious, at least for the present? If you do not mean as much as this, why do you make your circumstances your excuse at all? If you do mean this, then you are just as much mistaken as you can be. For despite your circumstances, God requires you to abandon your sin. Now, if your circumstances are so unusual that you cannot serve God in them, you must abandon them or lose your soul. If your circumstances are such that you can serve God in them, then do so at once.

But you say, "I can't get out of my circumstances." I reply, "You can; you can get out of the wickedness of them. If it is necessary in order to serve God, you can change them; and if not, you can repent and serve God in them."

A Peculiar Temperament

The sinner's next excuse is that his temperament is peculiar. "Oh," he says, "I am very nervous and excitable," or "My temperament is very sluggish—I seem to have no responsiveness toward anything." Now, what does God require? Does He require of you a level of responsiveness that is different from your own? Or does He require only that you should use what you have according to the law of love?

But such is the essence of a multitude of excuses. One person has too little excitability, another has too much, so neither feels he can possibly repent and serve God! What nonsense! A woman came to me and pleaded that she was naturally too excitable, dared not trust herself, and therefore could not repent. Another has the opposite trouble; she is too lethargic—rarely sheds a tear—and therefore can make nothing out of religion even if she tries. But does God require you to shed more tears than you are naturally able to shed? Or does He only require that you should serve Him? Certainly this is all. Serve Him with the very powers He has given you. Let your nerves be excitable; you can pour out that excitability into the heart of God! This is all that He requires. I know how to sympathize with that woman, for I know much about having a burning sensitivity. But does God require feeling and excitement, or only a perfect consecration of all our powers to Himself? Surely it is the latter.

Poor Health

"But," says another, "my health is so poor that I can't go to church and therefore can't be religious." Well, what does God require? Does He require you to go to all the meetings, whether you have the health for it or not? Infinitely far from it! If you are not able to go to a meeting, you can still give God your heart. If you cannot go in bad weather, be assured that God is infinitely the most reasonable Being that ever existed. He makes all due allowance for every circumstance.

Does He not know all your weaknesses? Indeed, He does. And do you suppose that He comes into your sickroom and criticizes you for not being able to go to church, or for not attempting when unable, and for not doing all in your sickness that you might do in health? No, not He; but He comes into your sickroom as a Father. He comes to pour out the deepest compassions of His heart in pity and in love. Why should you not respond to His loving-kindness? He comes to you and says, "Give Me your heart, My child." And now you reply, "I have no heart." Then He has nothing to ask of you; He thought you had a heart and that He had done enough to draw your heart in love and gratitude to Himself. He asks, "What can you find in all My dealings with you that is burdensome? If nothing, why do you bring forward these excuses for sin that accuse and condemn Me?"

45

A Hardened Heart

Another excuse says, "My heart is so hard that I cannot feel." This excuse is very common, both among believers and non-believers. In reality, it is only another form of the plea of inability. In fact, all the sinner's excuses amount to saying, "I am unable. I can't do what God requires." If the plea of a hard heart is any excuse at all, it must be on the ground of real inability.

But what is hardness of heart? Do you mean that you have such great apathy that you cannot muster any emotion? Or do you mean that you have no power to will or to act right? Now, on this point, it should be considered that the emotions are altogether involuntary. They come and go according to circumstances. Therefore, they are never required by the law of God and are not, properly speaking, either religion itself or any part of it. Hence, if by a hard heart you mean unresponsive emotions, you are talking about something that has no relevance to the subject. God asks you to yield your will and to consecrate it to Himself, and He asks this whether you have any feeling or not.

Real hardness of heart, as the phrase is used in the Bible, means "stubbornness of will." (See, for example, Mark 10:5 and Romans 2:5.) When you talk about a child who has a hard heart, you mean that his will is set in stubbornness against doing what his parents ask him to do. In connection with this, the child may have either much or little emotion. His emotions may be acute and thoroughly aroused, or they may be dormant. Yet in either case, the stubborn will may be there just the same.

Now, God complains of precisely the same kind of hardness of heart in the sinner. The sinner clings to his self-indulgence and will not relinquish it, and then he complains of hardness of heart. What would you think of a child who, when required to do a most reasonable thing, should say, "My heart is so hard, I can't yield." "Oh," he says, "my will is so set to have my own way that I cannot possibly yield to my father's authority."

This complaint is extremely common. Many sinners—those who have been often prayed with and wept over, who have been the subject of many convictions—make this excuse. Does the sinner really mean by this plea that he finds his will so obstinate that he cannot make up his mind to yield to God's claims? Does he mean this, and does he really intend to proclaim his own shame? Suppose you go to the devils in hell and press them with the claims of God. If they should reply, "Oh, my heart is so hard, I can't yield to God," what would be their meaning? Only this: "I am so obstinate, and my will is so set in sin, that I cannot for a moment indulge the thought of repentance." If the sinner is telling the truth of himself in the same words, he must mean the same thing that the devils mean. How he adds insult to injury by this declaration!

Suppose a child should say, "I cannot find it in my heart to love my father and my mother. My heart is so hard toward them that I never can love them. I can feel pleasure only in abusing them and trampling down their authority." What kind of plea is this? Does this not heap insult upon injury? Suppose a murderer is arraigned before the court and is permitted, before his sentence, to speak up and say why the sentence should not be passed. Suppose he should rise and say, "May it please the court, for a long time my heart has been as hard as a rock. I have murdered so many men, and have been in the practice so long, that I can kill a man without the least guilt of conscience. Indeed, I have such an insatiable thirst for blood that I cannot help murdering whenever I have a good opportunity. In fact, my heart is so hard that I find I like this business as well as any other."

Well, how long will the court listen to such a plea? "Stop right there," the judge would cry, "you infamous villain! We can hear no more of such pleas! Sheriff, bring in the gallows, and hang this man within these very walls of justice, for I will not leave the bench until I see him dead! He will murder us all here in this house if he can!"

Now what will we think of the sinner who says the same thing? "O God," he says, "my heart is so hard that I never can love You. I hate You so sincerely that I never can make up my mind to yield this heart to You in love and willing submission."

Sinners, many of you have pleaded, "My heart is so hard, I can't repent. I can't love and serve God." Go, write it down, and proclaim it to the universe. Make your boast of being so hardhearted that no claims of God can ever move you. I think if you were to make such a plea, you would not be half through before the whole universe would boo you from their presence and chase you from the face of these heavens until you would cry out for some rocks or mountains to hide you from their scathing rebukes! Their voice of indignation would rise up and ring along the arch of heaven like the roar of ten thousand tornadoes, and they would overwhelm you with unspeakable confusion and shame!

What? Do you insult and abuse the Great Jehovah? Do you condemn the very God who has watched over you in unspeakable love, fanned you with His gentle breezes in your sickness, feasted you at His own table? Can you not thank Him or even notice His providing hand? And when the sympathy of your Christian friends has pressed you with entreaties to repent, and they have made you a special subject of their prayers—when angels have wept over you, and unseen spirits have lifted their warning voices in your pathway to hell—you turn your face of brass toward Jehovah and tell Him your heart is so hard that you can't repent and don't care whether you ever do or not! You take hold of a spear and plunge it into the heart of the Crucified One, and then cry out, "I can't be sorry, not I; my heart is hard as stone! I don't care, and I will not repent." What a wretch you are, sinner, if this is your plea.

But what does your plea amount to? Only this— that your heart is fully set on doing evil. The Scriptures reveal your case most clearly: *"Because the sentence against an evil work is not executed speedily, therefore the heart of the sons of men is fully set in them to do evil"* (Eccl. 8:11). You stand before the Lord in this daring, blasphemous attitude, fully set in your heart upon doing evil.

A Wicked Heart

Another form of the same plea is, "My heart is so wicked, I can't yield." Some do not hesitate to declare this wickedness of heart. What do they mean by it? Do they mean that they are so hardened in sin, and so desperately wicked, that they will not bend? This is the only proper sense of their language, and this is the precise truth.

Since you, sinner, present this as your excuse, your purpose must be to blame this wickedness of heart upon God. Perhaps you do so covertly, but in truth you imply that God is involved in creating that wicked heart! This is it, and this is the whole of it. If it were not for the implication that God is at fault for your wicked heart, you would not have any interest in this excuse, and it would never escape your lips. Once again, this is only the plea of inability; but now it is coupled with its twin sister, original sin, which is said to be passed down in the created blood of the human race as the Creator's responsibility.

A Deceitful Heart

Another kindred plea is, "My heart is so deceitful." Suppose a man should make this excuse for deceiving his neighbor: "I can't help cheating you. I can't help lying to you and abusing you; my heart is so deceitful!" Would any man in his right mind ever suppose that this could be a defense or excuse for doing wrong? Never! Of course, unless the sinner wants to set forth his own guilt and condemn himself, he must intend this plea as some sort of justification. If it is for justification of himself, he is thereby casting the blame upon God. This is usually his intention. He does not mean to confess sincerely his own guilt; no, he charges the guilt of his deceitful heart upon God.

A Failed Attempt

Another sinner excuses himself with the plea, "I have tried to become a Christian. I have done all I can do; I have tried often, earnestly, and for a long time." You say you have tried to be a Christian. What is being a Christian? It is giving your heart to God. And what is giving your heart to God? Devoting your voluntary powers to Him, ceasing to live for yourself, and living for God. This is being a Christian—the state you say you have been trying to attain.

This excuse is quite common. And what is legitimately implied in this *trying* to be a Christian? It implies that there is a willingness to do your duty; that the heart, the *will,* is already right; and that the trying refers only to the outward efforts. For there is no sense whatsoever in a man's saying that he is trying to do what he has no intention of doing. The very statement implies that his will is not only in favor of but is also thoroughly and earnestly committed to attaining the end chosen.

Consequently, if a man tries to be a Christian, his heart is obedient to God, and his trying must be seen in his outward actions. Outward action is so connected with the will that it always follows the will unless the connection is broken. When this connection is broken, no sin accompanies our failure to perform the outward act. God does not hold us responsible.

Hence the sinner ought to mean by this plea, "I have obeyed God a long time. I have had a right heart, and I have tried sincerely to act only in ways that agree with Christian character." If this is true, then you have done your duty. But is this really what you mean when you say that you have tried to become a Christian? No, you say. Then what do you mean?

Suppose I should say to my son, "My son, why have you not done the thing I asked you to do?" "Oh, Father," he says, "I have tried," but he does not mean that he has ever intended to do it or that he has ever made up his mind to obey me. He only means, "I have been willing to try. I made up my mind to try to be willing." That is all! "Oh," he says, "I have brought myself to be willing to try to will to do it."

Similarly, you say, "I have tried to get religion." And what is religion, that you could not get it? How did you fail? God has said, "Give me your heart," and you have turned around and asked God to do it Himself. Or perhaps you have simply waited for Him to do it. He has commanded you to repent, and you have tried to get Him to repent for you. He said, *"Believe in the gospel"* (Mark 1:15), and you have only been thinking of getting Him to believe for you. No wonder you have tried for a long time in vain! How could it be otherwise? You have not been trying to do what God commanded you to do, but to get God to change His system of moral government and put Himself in your place to do the duty He demands of you. What a miserable perversion this is!

Now, what is the use of the whole plea of having tried to be a Christian? When it is understood as you intend it, you will see that it is utterly false. You will also see that it is a vulgar implication of the character of God.

You say, "Lord, I know I can't. I have tried all I can, and I know I cannot become a Christian. I am willing to get religion, but I cannot accomplish it."

Who, then, is to blame? Not yourself, according to your statement. Where, then, is the blame? Are you not placing the blame on God? But no one in the distant regions of the universe can ever believe such an accusation against his own Infinite Father! Of course, everyone will pronounce upon you the doom that you deserve.

Futility in Attempting

Another sinner excuses himself with the plea, "It will do no good to try." And what do you mean by this response? Do you mean that God will not pay well for service done for Him? Or do you mean that He will not forgive you if you do repent? Do you think, as some do, that you have sinned away your day of grace?

Well, suppose you have sinned away your day of grace. Is this any reason why you should go on in sin? Do you not believe that God is good and that He will forgive you if the good of the universe allows? Most certainly. Then is the impossibility of His forgiving you any reason why you should go on in sin forever, and forever rage against a God of infinite goodness? You believe Him to be compassionate and forgiving. Should you not therefore say, "I will at least stop sinning against such a God"?

There was a man who dreamed that he was going to hell. As he was parting with his brother—who was going, as his dream had it, to heaven—he said, "I am going down to hell, but I want you to tell God for me that I am greatly obliged to Him for ten thousand mercies that I never deserved; He has never done me the least injustice. Give Him my thanks for all the unmerited good He has done me." At this point, the man awoke and found himself bathed in tears of repentance and gratitude to his Father in heaven. Oh, if men would only act as reasonably as that man dreamed, it would be noble—it would be *right*. If only they would say, when they think they have sinned away their day of grace, "I know God is good. I will at least send Him my thanks, for He has done me no injustice"; if only they would take this course, they might have at least the satisfaction of feeling that it is a reasonable one in their circumstances. Sinner, will you at least thank God for what He has done for you?

Lack of Acceptance

Another sinner, when strongly urged to give his heart to Christ, says, "I have offered to give my heart to Christ, but He won't receive me. I have no evidence that He receives me or ever will." A young woman recently told me that she had offered to give her heart to the Lord, but He would not receive her. This was certainly a false accusation of Christ, for He has said, *"The one who comes to Me I will by no means cast out"* (John 6:37). You say, "I came and offered myself, and He would not receive me." Jesus Christ says, *"Behold, I stand at the door and knock. If anyone"*—not someone in particular, not some favored one—but if *any* person *"hears My voice and opens the door, I will come in to him"* (Rev. 3:20). And yet when you offered Him your heart, did He turn you away? Did He say, "Away, sinner; begone"? No, He never did, and He has said He never will do it. His own words are, *"The one who comes to Me I will by no means cast out"* (John 6:37). *"He who seeks finds, and to him who knocks it will be opened"* (Matt. 7:8).

But you say, "I have sought, and I did not find." Do you mean to say that Jesus Christ is a liar? Have you accused Him of this to His face? Do you solemnly affirm, "Lord, I did seek; I laid myself at Your gate and knocked, but all in vain"? And do you mean to present this excuse of yours as a solemn charge of falsehood against Jesus Christ and against God? This will be a serious matter with you before it is done.

No Salvation Available

But another says, "There is no salvation for me." Do you mean that Christ has made no atonement for you? The Scriptures say that He tasted death for everyone (Heb. 2:9). *"God so loved the world that He gave His only begotten Son, that whoever believes in Him should not perish but have everlasting life"* (John 3:16). Do you still affirm that there is no salvation provided and possible for you? Are you mourning all the way down to hell because you cannot possibly have salvation?

When the cup of salvation is placed to your lips, do you knock it away, saying, "This cannot be for me"? How do you *know* this? Can you prove it against the Word of God Himself? Stand up, then, and speak up, if you have such a charge against God. If you can, prove it to be true. Is there no hope? None at all? The difficulty is not that there is no salvation provided for and offered to you, but that there is no heart for it. *"Why is there in the hand of a fool the purchase price of wisdom, since he has no heart for it?"* (Prov. 17:16).

Inability to Change One's Own Heart

But perhaps you say in excuse, "I cannot change my own heart." Cannot? Suppose Adam had

55

made this excuse when God called him to repent after his first sin. "Make yourself a new heart and a right spirit," the Lord says to him. "I cannot change my own heart myself," replies Adam. His Maker then responds, "You changed your heart a few hours ago from holiness to sin. Will you now tell your Creator that you can't change it from sin to holiness?"

The sinner should consider that the change of heart is a voluntary thing. You must do it for yourself, or it will never be done. True, there is a sense in which God changes the heart, but it is only this: God influences the sinner to change, and then the sinner does it. The change is the sinner's own voluntary act.

More Conviction Needed

You say that you can't change your heart without more conviction. By this do you mean that you do not have enough knowledge of your duty and your sin? You cannot say this. You know both your sin and your duty. You know that you ought to consecrate yourself to God. What, then, do you mean? Can't you do what you know you ought to do? It is the old lie again—that shameless *"refuge of lies"* (Isa. 28:17)—that same foul dogma of inability. This new form of it implies that God is not willing to convict you enough to make it possible for you to repent. It claims that there is a work and a responsibility for God, and He will not do His work—will not bear His responsibility. Thus, unfortunately, you have no alternative but to go down to hell, and all because God will not do His part toward your salvation! Do you really believe this, sinner?

56

More of the Spirit Needed

Again, you say in excuse that you must first have more of the Spirit, and yet you resist the Spirit every day. God offers you His Spirit—more than this, God bestows His Spirit upon you. But you resist Him. What, then, do you mean when you pretend to need more of the Spirit's influence?

The truth is, you do not want it. You only want to make it appear that God does not do His part to help you to repent, and that, because you can't repent without His help, the blame of your impenitence rests on God. It is only another *"refuge of lies"*—another form of the old slander against God that says, "He has made me unable and won't help me out of my inability."

God's Responsibility

The sinner also excuses himself by saying, "God must change my heart." But in the sense in which God requires you to do it, He cannot do it Himself. God changes the heart only in the sense of persuading you to do it. When a man changes his political views, he might say, "This friend of mine changed my heart; he convinced me of his views." But this does not imply that the man did not change his own mind. The plain meaning is that the one persuaded and the other yielded.

This excuse made by the sinner implies that there is something more for God to do before the sinner can become religious. I have heard many so-called believers take this very stance. Yes, thousands of Christian ministers, too, have said to the sinner, "Wait for God. He will change your heart in His own good time. You can't do it yourself, and all that you can do is to put yourself in the way for the Lord to change your heart. When this time comes, He will give you a new heart—perhaps even while you are asleep, in a state of unconsciousness. God is sovereign in this matter and does His own work in His own way."

Thus they teach, filling the mouth of the sinner with excuses and making his heart hard as a rock and set against the real claims of God upon his conscience.

Inability to Live as a Christian

The sinner pleads, again, "I couldn't live a Christian life even if I were to become a Christian. It is unreasonable for me to expect to succeed where I see so many fail." I recall the case of a man who said, "It is of no use for me to repent and be a Christian, for it is altogether irrational for me to expect to do better than others have done before me." Sinners who make this excuse come forward very modestly and tell God, "I am very humble. You see, Lord, that I have a very low opinion of myself. I am so zealous of Your honor, and so afraid that I will bring disgrace upon Your cause, that it does not seem at all best for me to think of becoming a Christian, for I have such a horror of dishonoring Your name."

And what then? "Therefore, I will go on sinning and trampling the blessed Gospel under my feet. (See Hebrews 10:29.) I will persecute You, O my God, and make war on Your cause, for it is better by far not to profess religion than to profess and then disgrace my profession." What logic! Yet this is a fair specimen of the absurdity of the sinner's excuses.

This excuse assumes that there is not enough grace provided and offered to sustain the soul in the Christian life. You will recall that the doctrine taught by the Confession of Faith states that it is irrational to expect that we can, by any grace received in this life, perfectly obey the law of God. But what a lie to say there is not enough grace and help afforded by God! And this is taught as *Bible theology!* Away with such teaching to the hellish pit from which it came!

What! Is God so weak that He can't hold up the soul that casts itself on Him? Or is He so tightfisted in bestowing His gracious aid that it must be expected always to fall short of meeting the needs of His children? So you seem to think. Is it so hard to persuade the Lord to give you a particle of grace? Can you not get enough grace to live a Christian life with honor? What is this but accusing God of withholding sufficient grace?

But what does the Word of God say? We read that

> *God, determining to show more abundantly to the heirs of promise the immutability of His counsel, confirmed it by an oath, that by two immutable things, in which it is impossible for God to lie, we might have strong consolation, who have fled for refuge to lay hold of the hope set before us.*   *(Heb. 6:17–18)*

You say, however, "If I were to lay hold of this hope, I would fail for lack of grace. I could have no *'consolation'* in resting on the Word of Him who cannot lie. The oath of the immutable God can never suffice for me."

In this way, you contradict the Word of God, and you make up a miserably slim and guilty apology for your impenitence.

A Dark, Mysterious Subject

Another excuse claims that this is a very dark, mysterious subject. "This matter of faith and regeneration," says the sinner, "I can't understand it."

Sinner, did you ever meet the Lord with this objection, and say, "Lord, You have required me to do things that I can't understand"? You know that you can understand well enough that you are a sinner, that Christ died for you, and that you must believe on Him, turn away from your sins, and repent. (See Ezekiel 14:6.) All this is so plain that *"whoever walks the road, although a fool, shall not go astray"* (Isa. 35:8). Your plea, therefore, is as false as it is foul. It is nothing better than a degrading lie about God!

Lack of Faith

But you say, "I can't believe." Don't you mean that you can't believe a God of infinite truthfulness as much as you can believe your fellowman? Are you implying that God asks you to believe things that are really too hard to believe—things so revolting to your reason that you cannot believe them on any testimony that even God Himself can offer?

Do you expect to win this case against God? Do you even believe the first point of it yourself?

But you say again that you can't fully believe these things. You know these things to be true, but you can't fully believe. You can't realize that the Bible is true, that God does offer to forgive, that salvation is actually provided and placed within your reach. What help can there be for a case like yours? What can make these truths more certain to you? But, from what you have said, you do not need more evidence. Why not, then, act on what you already know to be the truth? What more can you ask?

Do you ever take your case before God and say, "O Lord, You say that Christ died for me, but I can't fully realize that it is so. Therefore, Lord, I can't possibly embrace Him as my Savior"? Would this be a rational excuse?

Unwilling to Repent

But you also plead that you can't repent. You say you can't be sorry that you have abused God. You can't make up your mind now to turn away from all sin. If this is really so, then you cannot make up your mind to obey God, and you may as well make up your mind to go to hell. There is no alternative!

But at any rate, you say you can't become a Christian now. You intend to be converted sometime, but you can't make up your mind to do it now. Well, God requires it now, and of course you must yield or deal with the consequences.

But do you say, "I can't do it now"? Then God is very much to blame for asking it of you. If, however, the truth is that you can do it now, then the lie is on your side, and it is a most infamous and abusive lie against your Maker.

Adding Insult to Injury

Any plea that reflects poorly upon the court or the lawgiver only makes the original crime worse. It is always so in all courts of law, and so it must be between the sinner and his infinite Lawgiver and Judge.

The same is true of any plea made in self-justification. If it is false, it is considered to be an aggravation of the crime charged. When this happens, it is thought to add fresh insult and wrong. For a criminal to come and put his lie upon the records of the court—to declare what he knows to be false—nothing can damage his case so fearfully as this.

On the other hand, when a man standing before the court appears to be honest and confesses his guilt, the judge, if he has any discretion in the case, reduces his sentence to the lowest point possible. But if the criminal resorts to dodging—if he lies and evades the question—then you will see the strong arm of the law come down upon him. The judge comes forth in all the thunders of judicial majesty and terror and feels that he must not spare his victim. Why? The man has lied before the court of justice itself. The man sets himself against all law, and he must be put down, or law itself is put down.

It is truly abominable for the sinner to abuse God and then attempt to excuse himself for it. But this is only the way that the guilty have always gone. Adam and Eve in the Garden fled and hid themselves when they heard the voice of the Lord approaching. And what had they done? The Lord called them out and began to question them: "Adam, what have you done? Have you eaten of the forbidden tree in the center of the Garden?" Adam quailed, but immediately tried to excuse himself: *"The woman whom You gave to be with me, she gave me of the tree, and I ate"* (Gen. 3:12). He said that God gave him his tempter! According to Adam's excuse, God was chiefly to blame in the transaction.

Next He turned to the woman to ask, *"What is this you have done?"* (v. 13). She, too, had an excuse: *"The serpent deceived me, and I ate"* (v. 13). Ah, this perpetual shuffling of the blame back upon God! It has been kept up through the long line of Adam's imitators, down to this very day. For six thousand years, God has been hearing it, and still the world is spared, and the vengeance of God has not yet burst forth to smite all His guilty accusers to hell! Oh, what patience there is in God! And who has ever abused His patience and insulted Him by his excuses more than sinners?

REMARKS

1. No sinner under the light of the Gospel lives a single hour in sin without some excuse, either implied or expressed, by which he justifies himself. It seems to be a law of man's intelligent nature that, when accused of wrong, either by his conscience or by any other agent, he must either confess or justify himself. The latter is the course taken by all impenitent sinners.

Thus we see why sinners have so much opportunity for excuses, and why they find it convenient to have such a great variety of them. It is remarkable with what ease they fly from one to another, as if these refuges of lies might make up in number what they lack in strength. They are aware that not one of all the multitude of excuses is valid. Yet when questioned about one, they fly to another; and when driven from all of them in succession, they are ready to come back and fight the same argument all over again. It is so hard for them to abandon all excuses and admit the humbling truth that they themselves are all wrong and God is all truth.

Hence, it becomes the great business of a minister of the Gospel to search out and expose the sinner's excuses; to go all around and, if possible, demolish the sinner's refuges of lies; and to lay his heart open to the arrows of truth.

2. Excuses make repentance impossible, for excuses are self-justifications, and who does not know that self-justification is the very opposite of confession and repentance? To seek and embrace excuses, therefore, is to place oneself at the farthest possible point from repentance.

Of course, the self-excusing sinner makes it impossible for God to forgive him. He places the Deity in such a position toward himself, and he places himself in such an attitude toward the government of God, that his forgiveness would be destructive to the throne of God. What would heaven say—and hell and earth besides—if God were to forgive a sinner while he, by his excuses, is justifying himself and condemning his Maker?

3. Sinners should lay all their excuses at once before God. Surely this is most reasonable. Suppose that a man owes me a large sum of money and that he has a reasonable excuse for not paying the debt. He should come to me and try to get me to understand the whole case. Perhaps he will satisfy me that his views are right.

Now, sinner, have you ever done this in regard to God? Why not? Have you ever brought up even one excuse before the Lord, saying, "You require me to be holy, but I can't be. Lord, I have a good excuse for not obeying You"? No, sinner; you are not in the habit of doing this—you probably have not done this even once in your whole life. In fact, you have no good reason to carry your excuses before God, for you do not have one that you yourself believe to be good for anything except to answer the purpose of a *"refuge of lies"* (Isa. 28:17). Your excuses won't stand the ordeal of your own reason and conscience. How, then, can you hope they will stand before the searching eye of Jehovah? The fact that you never come to God with your excuses shows that you have no confidence in them.

4. What infinite madness to rest on excuses that you dare not bring before God! How can you stand before God in the Judgment if your excuses are so poor that you cannot seriously think of bringing one of them before God in this world? O sinner, that coming Day will be far more searching and awful than anything you have seen yet. See that dense mass of sinners gathering before the Great White Throne. As far as the eye can see, they come surging up, a countless throng. Now, as they stand, the awful trumpet of God summons them forward to bring forth their excuses for sin: "Sinners—any one of you, or all of you—can you tell Me why sentence should not be passed on you?"

Where are all those excuses you were once so free and bold to make? Where are they all? Why don't you make them now? God waits; He listens; there is silence in heaven, all through the congregated throng, for half an hour. (See Revelation 8:1.) It is an awful silence that may be felt; there is not a word—not a moving lip among the gathered myriads of sinners there. Now the great and dreadful Judge arises and lets loose His thunders. Oh, see the waves of dire damnation roll over the masses of self-condemned sinners! Did you ever see a judge rise from his bench in court to pass the sentence of death on a criminal? The poor man reels—there is no longer any strength in him, for death is on him, and his last hope has perished!

O sinner, fear the Day when that sentence from the awe-inspiring throne falls on you! Your excuses will be like millstones around your neck as you plunge down the sides of the pit to the lowest hell!

5. Sinners don't need their excuses. God does not ask for even one. He does not require you to justify yourself—not at all. If you needed them for your salvation, I could sympathize with you, and certainly I would help you if I could. But you don't need them. Your salvation does not depend on your successful self-vindication. You need not rack your brain for excuses. It is better to say, "I don't want them; I do not have one that is worth a straw."

You could also better say, "I am wicked. God knows this to be the truth, and it would be futile for me to attempt to conceal it. I am wicked, and if I ever live, it must be on simple mercy!"

I can recall very well the year I lived on excuses, and how long it was before I gave them up. I had never heard a minister preach on the subject. By my experience, however, I found that my excuses and lies were the obstacles standing in the way of my conversion. As soon as I let them go entirely, I found the gate of mercy wide open. And so would you, sinner.

6. Sinners ought to be ashamed of their excuses and repent of them. Perhaps you have not always seen this as plainly as you may now. With the light now before you, it would suit you to beware. See to it that you never make another excuse, unless you intend to abuse God in the most horrible manner. Nothing can be a more serious abomination in the sight of God than excuses made by a sinner who knows they are utterly false and blasphemous. Sinner, you ought to repent of the insult you have already offered to God, lest you find yourself thrust away from the gate of mercy.

7. You acknowledge your obligation, and of course this makes it impossible for you to make excuses. If any one of you has a good excuse for disobeying God, you are no longer under obligation to obey. But since you are compelled to acknowledge your obligation, you are also compelled to relinquish your excuses.

8. Inasmuch as you acknowledge your obligation, if you still plead excuses, you insult God to His face. You insult Him by accusing Him of infinite tyranny.

Now, what is to be made of all this? Are you ready to say, "From now on I will cease from all my excuses, now and forever, and God will have my whole heart"? Or will you begin to hunt up some new excuse? Do you say, "Let me think about it first. Don't urge me to yield to God here on the spot. Let me think about it, and then I will"? Do you say this? Are you aware of how tender this moment is—how critical this passing hour is? Remember, it is not I who press this claim upon you, but it is God. God Himself commands you to repent today—*this hour*. You know your duty; you know what religion is— what it is to give God your heart. And now I come to the final question: Will you do it? Will you abandon all your excuses, fall as a self-condemned sinner before a God of love, and yield yourself to Him—your heart and your whole being, now and forever? Will you come?

Three

The Sinner's Excuses
Answered

*Elihu also proceeded and said: "Bear with me a little,
and I will show you that there are yet words to speak
on God's behalf. I will fetch my knowledge from afar; I
will ascribe righteousness to my Maker."*
—Job 36:1–3

E lihu was present and heard the controversy between Job and his friends. These friends maintained that God's dealings with Job proved him
to be wicked. Job denied this and insisted that we
cannot judge men to be good or bad from God's
providential dealings with them, because facts show
that the present world is not one of rewards and
punishments. They, however, regarded this as taking sides with the wicked and did not hesitate to accuse Job of doing this.

Elihu had previously said, "My desire is that Job
may be tried in regard to what he has said of wicked
men." (See Job 34:36.) But before the discussion
closed, he saw that Job had frustrated his three
friends, maintaining unanswerably that it was not
because of any hypocrisy or special guilt that he was
so unusually scourged. Yet, plainly, even Job did not
have the key to explain God's dealings with him. To

him it was still a mystery. He did not see that God might have been seeking to test and discipline his piety, or even to make an example of his integrity and submissiveness with which to baffle the Devil.

Elihu's intention was to speak on God's behalf and to ascribe righteousness to his Maker. My present objective is to do the same in regard to sinners who refuse to repent and who complain of God's ways. But before I proceed, let me bring up a particular fact.

A few years ago, in my labors as an evangelist, I became acquainted with a man prominent in his town for his intelligence. This man's two successive wives were daughters of old-school Presbyterian clergymen. Through them he had received many books to read on religious subjects, which they and their friends thought would do him good, but which failed to do him any good at all. He denied the inspiration of the Bible, and he did so on grounds that he felt those books did not rule out. Indeed, they only served to intensify his objections.

When I came into the town, his wife was very anxious that I should see and converse with him. I went to the couple's home, and his wife sent for him to come and see the new minister. To this he replied that he was sure the minister could do him no good, since he had conversed with so many and had found no light on the points that so much bewildered him. But when she urgently pleaded with him, he consented for her sake to meet with me.

At the outset I said to him, "Don't think that I have come here to quarrel with you and to provoke a dispute. I only wish at your wife's request to converse with you, if you are willing, upon the great subject of divine revelation." He indicated his pleasure to have such a conversation, and accordingly I asked him to briefly state his position. He replied, "I acknowledge the truths of natural religion and believe most fully in the immortality of the soul, but not in the inspiration of the Scriptures. I am a Deist." So I asked, "On what grounds do you deny the inspiration of the Bible?" He said, "I know it cannot be true." "How do you know that?" "It contradicts the affirmations of my reason. You and I both acknowledge that God created my nature, both physical and moral. Here is a book, said to be from God, but it contradicts my nature. I therefore know it cannot be from God."

This reply, of course, opened the door for me. I was able to draw from him the particular points of his objection to the Bible as teaching what contradicted his nature. In the following pages of this chapter, I will present these points and my reply to them.

Is God Unjust?

This man's first objection was that the Bible cannot be true because it represents God as unjust. He said to me, "I have certain convictions as to what is just and unjust. The Bible goes against these convictions. It represents God as creating men and then condemning them for someone else's sin."

"Indeed, does it? Where does it say this?" I questioned. "Doesn't it?" he asked, and I replied, "No." "Are you a Presbyterian?" he said. "Yes." He then began to quote the catechism. "Stop, stop," I said, "that is not the Bible. That is only a human catechism." "True," he said, "but doesn't the Bible connect the universal sin of the race with the sin of

Adam?" "Yes, it does in a particular way, but it is quite essential to our purpose to understand in *what* way. The Bible makes this connection incidental, not direct; it always represents the condemned sinner as really sinning himself, and as condemned for his own sin."

"But," he continued, "children do suffer for their father's sins." "Yes, in a certain sense it is so, and must be so. Do you not see with your own eyes, everywhere, that children must suffer for the sins of their parents and also be blessed by the piety of their parents? You see this, and you find no fault with it. You see that children must be implicated in the good or bad conduct of their parents; their relationship as children makes this absolutely unavoidable. Is it not wise and good that the happiness or misery of children should depend on their parents, and thus become one of the strongest possible motives to parents to train them up in virtue? Yet it is true that the son is never rewarded or punished for his parents' sins. The evil that befalls him through his connection with his parents is always for instruction, not punishment."

Does God Condemn Man's Sinful Nature?

The man then said to me, "The Bible certainly represents God as creating men sinners, and as condemning them for their sinful nature." "No," I replied, "the Bible defines sin as voluntary transgression of the law, and it is absurd to suppose that a *nature* can be a voluntary transgressor. Besides, it is impossible for God to have made a sinful nature. And even if it were possible, it would still be *morally* impossible for Him to do it. He could not do it for the same reason that He cannot sin; He is infinite goodness."

In harmony with this is the fact that the Bible never represents God as condemning men for their nature, either here or at the Judgment. Nowhere in the Bible is there the least suggestion that God holds men responsible for their created nature, but only for the vile and stubborn abuse of their nature. Other views of this matter, differing from this, are not the Bible, but are only false glosses put upon it—usually by those whose philosophy has led them into absurd interpretations. Throughout the Bible, men are condemned only for their voluntary sins and are required to repent of these sins, and only of these. Indeed, there cannot possibly be any other sins than these.

Is God Cruel?

Another objection is that the Bible represents God as being cruel, inasmuch as He commanded the Jews to wage a war of extermination against the ancient Canaanites.

But why should this be called cruel? The Bible explicitly informs us that God commanded this action because of their awful wickedness. They were too horribly wicked to live. God could not allow them to defile the earth and corrupt society. Thus, He arose in His zeal for human welfare and commanded to wash the land clean of such unutterable abominations. The good of the human race demanded it. Was this cruel? No, truly this was simply benevolent. It was one of the highest acts of benevolence to strike down such a race and sweep them from the face of the earth. To employ the Jews as His executioners, allowing them to understand distinctly *why* He commanded them to do it, was putting them in a position to derive the highest moral benefit from the transaction. In no other way could they have been so solemnly impressed with the holy justice of Jehovah. Will any man find fault with God for this? No one can reasonably do so.

Does the Bible Allow Slavery?

"But the Bible allows slavery," says the sinner. What? The Bible allows slavery? In what sense does the Bible allow it, and under what circumstances? What kind of slavery? These are all very important questions if we wish to know the certainty and the meaning of the things we say.

The Bible does indeed say that the Jews, in the case of captives taken in war, were permitted to exchange death for servitude. When the customs of existing nations put captives taken in war to death, God authorized the Jews in certain cases to spare their captives and employ them as servants. By this means, they were taken out from among idolatrous nations and brought into contact with the worship and ordinances of the true God. Who will call this cruel? Jewish servitude was not American slavery, nor even an approximation of it.

Is God Unmerciful?

Again, it is objected that God is unmerciful, vindictive, and implacable. The gentleman to whom I have alluded said, "I don't believe the Bible is from God when it represents Him as so vindictive and implacable that He would not forgive sin until He had first taken measures to kill His own Son."

Now, it was by no means unnatural for this man to think so, under the teaching he had received. I myself had once felt the same way; this very objection had bewildered me. But I afterward saw the answer so plainly that it left nothing more to be desired. Indeed, the answer is exceedingly plain. It was not a merciless disposition in God that led Him to require the death of Christ as the ground of forgiveness. It was simply His benevolent regard for the safety and blessedness of His kingdom. He knew very well that it was unsafe to forgive sin without such atonement.

Indeed, this was the strongest possible display of a forgiving character, to agree to the sacrifice of His Son for this purpose. He loved His Son and certainly would not inflict one needless pang upon Him. He also loved a sinning race and saw the depth of the ruin toward which they were rushing. Therefore, He longed to forgive them and to prepare a way in which He could do so with safety. He only desired to avoid all misunderstanding. To forgive without the kind of atonement that would adequately express His abhorrence of sin would leave the intelligent universe to think that He did not care how much any being would sin. This would not do.

Let it also be considered that the giving up of Jesus Christ was only a voluntary offering on God's part to sustain law, so that He could forgive without peril to His government. Jesus was not in any sense punished; He volunteered to suffer for sinners so that they might be freed from the governmental necessity of suffering. Was not mercy manifested in this? Certainly. How could it be manifested more notably?

Does God Require the Impossible?

"But," says the objector, "God is unjust because He requires the impossible, on pain of eternal death."

Does He, indeed? Then where is this stated in the law or in the Gospel? When we look at the law and the Gospel together, we have the sum of all God's requirements. In what part of either law or Gospel do you find the precept that requires impossibilities? Is it in the law? The law says only, *"You shall love the LORD your God with all your heart"* (Deut. 6:5)—not with another man's heart, but simply with your own. Read on still further: *"and with all your strength"* (v. 5)—not with the strength of an angel, not with the strength of any other being than yourself, but only with the amount of strength that you actually have for the time being. The demands of the law, you see, exactly match your abilities— nothing more and nothing else.

"Indeed," said the gentleman with whom I was conversing, "this is a new view of the subject." But is this not just as it should be? Doesn't the law require us to do only what we can and nothing more? How can anyone say that the law requires of us impossible service—things we have no power to do?

"But," the man said, "is it not true that 'no mere man since the Fall has been able wholly to keep the commandments of God, but daily breaks them in thought, word, and deed'?"

My friend, that is catechism, not Bible. We must be careful not to attribute to the Bible everything that human catechisms have said. The Bible only requires you to consecrate to God what strength and powers you actually have. It is by no means responsible for the idea that God requires of man more than he can do. In truth, the Bible nowhere credits God with such an unreasonable and cruel request. No wonder the human mind rebels against such a view of God's law! If any human law were to require impossibilities, there could be no end to the criticisms that would fall upon it. No human mind could possibly approve of such a law. Nor can it be supposed that God can reasonably act on principles that would disgrace and ruin any human government.

"But," continued the gentleman, "here is another objection. The Bible represents men as unable to believe the Gospel unless they are drawn by God, for it reads, *'No one can come to Me unless the Father who sent Me draws him'* (John 6:44). Yet sinners are required to believe on pain of damnation. How is this?"

In reply, I must first say that in this Scripture, Christ referred to *drawing* by means of teaching or instruction. To confirm this, I point you to the following verse, where He appealed to the ancient Scriptures: *"It is written in the prophets, 'And they shall all be taught by God'"* (v. 45). Without this teaching, then, no one can come. They must know Christ before they can come to Him in faith. They cannot believe until they know what to believe. In this sense of coming, untaught heathen are not required to come.

God never requires any to come who have not been taught. Once taught, they are bound to come, are required to come, and are without excuse if they refuse.

"But," the gentleman replied, "the Bible does really teach that men cannot serve the Lord, and yet it holds them responsible for doing it. Joshua said to all the people, *'You cannot serve the LORD, for He is a holy God'* (Josh. 24:19)."

Let us look at this closely. Joshua had called all the people together and had laid before them their obligation to serve the Lord their God. When they all said readily and with little serious consideration that they would, Joshua replied, *"You cannot serve the LORD, for He is a holy God. He is a jealous God; He will not forgive your transgressions nor your sins"* (v. 19). What did he mean? Clearly, he meant, "You cannot serve God because you have not fully abandoned your sins. You cannot get along with a God so holy and so jealous unless you give up sinning. You cannot serve God with a selfish heart. You cannot please Him until you really renounce your sins altogether. You must begin by making new hearts for yourselves."

Undoubtedly, Joshua saw that they had not given up their sins, had not really begun to serve God at all, and did not even understand the first principles of true religion. This is why he seemed to rebuff them so suddenly. It is as if he wanted to say, "Stop! You must go back and begin by utterly putting away all your sins. You cannot serve a holy and jealous God in any other way, for He will not go along with you as His people if you persist in sinning against Him."

It is a gross perversion of the Bible to make it mean that men have no power to do what God requires. Although the words *can* and *cannot* are used here, these words should be interpreted according to the nature of the subject. All reasonable men understand this principle in the common use of language. The Bible always uses the language of common life and in the way of common usage. Hence, it should be thus interpreted.

When it is said that Joseph's brothers *"hated him and could not speak peaceably to him"* (Gen. 37:4), the meaning is not that their tongues and vocal cords could not articulate kind words. Rather, it points us to a difficulty in their hearts. They hated him so badly they could not speak pleasantly. Nor do the Scriptures assume that they could not at once subdue this hatred and treat Joseph as brother should treat brother. The writers of the sacred Scriptures are the last men in the world to defend sin in this manner.

There is also the case of the angels sent to hurry Lot out of guilty Sodom. One said, *"Hurry, escape there* [to Zoar]. *For I cannot do anything until you arrive there"* (Gen. 19:22). Does this mean that the Almighty God had no power to overwhelm Sodom as long as Lot was in it? Certainly not. It meant only that it was His purpose not to destroy the city until Lot was out. All men use language this way in common life. You go into a store and say to the merchant, "Can you single-handedly lift a ton of your goods at once?" He will say no. But if you asked, "Can you sell me that piece of cloth for a penny a yard?" would this *can* mean the same as the other? By no means. But how do you detect the difference?

How is it that you know so readily which is the physical *cannot* and which the moral? The nature of the subject tells you.

But regarding the Scriptures, you say that the same word should always mean the same thing. Well, it does not, in any language ever yet spoken by man. Yet there is no difficulty in understanding even the most imperfect of human languages if men are honest in speaking, are honest in hearing, and will use their common sense. They intuitively interpret language according to the nature of the subject spoken of.

The Bible always assumes that sinners cannot do right and please God with a wicked heart. It always takes the position that God abhors hypocrisy, that He cannot be satisfied with mere forms and professions of service when the heart is not in it. Thus, all acceptable service must begin with making a new and sincere heart. (See Ezekiel 18:31 KJV.)

Can Sinners Make New Hearts for Themselves?

"But here is another difficulty," said the man. "Can I make a new heart for myself?"

Yes, and you would not doubt that you could if you only understood what the language means.

Picture Adam and Eve in the Garden. What were their hearts? Did God create them? No; it is not possible that He did, for a heart in this sense is not the subject of physical creation. When God made Adam, giving him all the capacities for acting morally, he had no heart—good or bad—until he came to act morally. When did Adam first have a moral heart? When he first awoke to moral consciousness and gave his heart to God, when he first saw God manifested, when he put confidence in Him as his Father and yielded up his heart to Him in love and obedience. Notice that he first had this holy heart because he yielded up his will to God in entire consecration. This was his first holy heart.

But, in time, the hour of temptation came, enticing him to withdraw his heart from God and turn to pleasing himself. The Tempter said to Eve, *"You will not surely die"* (Gen. 3:4). Is that so? Then he raised a question either about whether God had really threatened death for sin, or whether it was just to do so. In either case, he raised a question about obedience and opened the heart to temptation.

Then the fruit came before her mind. It was pleasing to the eye and seemed good for food (v. 6). Her appetite craved the indulgence. Then, when she heard that the fruit was able to *"make one wise"* (v. 6) and that by eating it she might *"be like God, knowing good and evil"* (v. 5), this appealed to her curiosity. Yielding to this temptation and making up her mind to please herself, she made herself a new heart of sin; she changed her heart from holiness to sin, and she fell from her first moral position. When Adam yielded to temptation, he made the same change in his heart; he gave himself up to selfishness and sin. This accounts for all future acts of selfishness.

Picture Adam and Eve being again brought before God. God says to Adam, "Give Me your heart. Change your heart." "What!" says Adam. "I cannot change my own heart!" But God replies, "But it was only yesterday that you changed your own heart from holiness to sin. Why can't you change it back?"

It is the same in all cases. Changing the ruling preference, the governing purpose of the mind, is the thing. Who can say, "I cannot do that"? Can't you do this? Can't you give yourself to God?

The reason you cannot please God in your outward acts is that your governing purpose is not right. When your leading motive is wrong, everything you do is selfish, because it is all done for the single purpose of pleasing yourself. You do nothing for the sake of pleasing God or with the governing purpose of doing His holy will. Therefore, everything you do, even your religious duties, only displeases God. If the Bible had anywhere represented God as being pleased with your hypocritical services, it would be proven false, for this is perfectly impossible.

But you say that the Bible requires you to begin with the inner man—with the heart—and you say that you cannot reach your own heart in order to change it.

Indeed, you are entirely mistaken. This is the one thing that is most entirely within your power. Of all things, this is the thing that you can do most certainly—that is most absolutely within your power. If God had made your salvation dependent upon your walking across a room, you might not be able to do it. Or if He had made it dependent on lifting your eyelids or rising from your seat, or the least movement of your muscles, you might be utterly unable to do it. You could *want* to perform the required motion, and you could try, but the muscles might have no power to act.

You often think that if God had only made your salvation dependent on some motions of your muscles, it would have been so easy—if He had only asked you to control the outside. But you say, "How can I control the inside?" The inside is the very thing you can move and control. If it had been the outside, you might try until you die and not be able to move a muscle, even if you faced the penalty of an eternal hell. But now, because God only says, "Change your will," everything is brought within your control. This is just the thing you always *can* do; you can always move your will. You can always give your heart, by your own choice.

Where, then, is your difficulty and objection? God requires you to act with your freedom, to exercise the powers of free and voluntary action that He has given you. He asks you to put your hand on the fountainhead of all your own power, to act just where your central power lies—where you *always* have power as long as you have a rational mind and a moral nature. Your liberty does not lie in the power to move your muscles at will, for the connection between your muscles and your will may be broken. Therefore, God does not require you to perform any particular movement of the muscles, but only to change your will. This, compared with all other things, is something you can always do, and can do more surely than anything else.

The whole question is, Will you please God or yourself? Will you give your heart to Him, or will you give it to your own selfish enjoyment? What are the ultimate purposes that govern you? As long as you give your heart to selfish pleasure and withhold it from God, it will be perfectly natural for you to sin.

This is precisely the reason that it is so natural for sinners to sin. It is because the will, the heart, is set upon it, and all they have to do is to carry out this ruling propensity and purpose. But, if you would just change this governing purpose, you will find obedience equally natural and equally easy. It will then become natural to please God in everything. Right now, pleasing yourself is natural enough. Why? Because you are dedicated to pleasing yourself. But if you change this purpose—if you dedicate yourself to something new and totally opposite, reverse the committed heart, and let it be for God and not for self—then all duty will be easy for the same reason that all sin is so easy now.

Far from being true that you are unable to make your heart new, the fact is you would long ago have done it if you had not resisted God in His efforts to move you to repentance. Have you not often resisted God's Spirit? Indeed, you know you have. Your convictions that you *ought* to live for God were so clear that you had to resist every appeal of your own conscience, march right in the face of known duty, and press your way along directly against God. If you had only listened to the voice of your reason and to the demands of your conscience, you would have had a new heart long ago. But you resisted God when He tried to persuade you to have a new heart.

Sinner, how strong you have been in resisting God! How strong in resisting every consideration addressed to your mind and to your reason! How strangely you have listened to the considerations for sinning! Oh, the miserable petty things—tell me, what were they? Suppose Christ should question you and ask, "What is there on earth, that you should love it so well? What is there in sin, that you should prize it above My favor and My love? What are those little indulgences, those very small things that always die out as soon as they are used?" *"Vanity of vanities, all is vanity"* (Eccl. 1:2).

This is utterly contemptible! You have been holding on to sin with no reasonable motive for doing so. Consider what motives you have fought against and resisted—motives of almost infinite force! Think of the motives resulting from God's law—so excellent in itself, but so dreadful in its penalties against transgressors. Then think of God's infinite love in the Gospel, how He opened the life-tides of His great heart and let blessings flow with fullness! Yet consider how, despite this love, you have abused your God exceedingly. You have gone on as if the motivations to sin were all-persuasive, and as if sin's promises of good were more reliable than God's. When God spread out before you the glories of heaven, made all attractive and delightful in the beauties of holiness, you coolly replied, "Earth is far better! Give me earth while I can have it, and heaven only when I can have earth no longer!" O sinner, you would have been converted long ago if you had not opposed God and trodden underfoot His invitations and His appeals! (See Hebrews 10:29.)

This moral agency—how great its power! How important, therefore, must be its responsibilities! When God is pouring forth influences in waves of light and power, with a kind of moral omnipotence, you resist and withstand it all—as if you could do anything you pleased, in spite of God! As if His influence were almost utterly powerless to move your heart from its fixed intention to sin!

Does it require great strength to lay down your weapons? One would suppose it requires great strength to resist and to fight. And so you put forth your great strength in fighting against God, and would gladly believe that you do not have enough strength to lay your weapons down! Oh, the absurdity of sin and of the sinner's defense for sinning!

But you say, "I must have the Holy Spirit." I answer, "Yes, but only to overcome your voluntary opposition. That is all."

After I had gone over this ground with my friend, as I have already explained, he became very much agitated. The sweat started from every pore; his feelings overcame him; he dropped his head down upon his knees, buried in the most intense thought and full of emotion. I got up and went to the meeting at the church. After it had progressed awhile, he came in. How changed he was! He said, "Dear wife, I don't know what has become of my unbelief. I ought to be sent to hell! What charges I have been making against God! And yet with what amazing mercy did my God bear with me and let me live!" In fact, he found he had been all wrong, and he humbled himself and became as a little child before God. (See Matthew 18:4.)

You, too, sinner, know you ought to live for God, yet you have not been doing so. You know that Jesus made Himself an offering to the injured dignity of the law that you violated, yet you have rejected Him. He gave Himself as a voluntary offering, not to suffer the penalty of the law, but as your legal Substitute. Will He have done all this in vain? Do you say, "Oh, I'm so prejudiced against God and the Bible!" What, so prejudiced that you will not repent? How horrible! Let it suffice that you have played the fool so long and erred so exceedingly. It has been all wrong! At once return and devote yourself to God. Why should you live for yourself at all? You can get no good by doing so!

Come to God—He is so easily pleased! It is so much easier to please Him than to please and satisfy yourself. A little child can please Him. Children often have the most delightful piety, because it is so simple-hearted. They know what to do to please God, and, honestly intending to please Him, they cannot fail. No matter how simple-hearted they are, if they intend to please God, they surely will. Can you not at least honestly choose and aim to please God?

Four

On Refuges of Lies

*Also I will make justice the measuring line,
and righteousness the plummet; the hail will
sweep away the refuge of lies, and the waters will
overflow the hiding place.*
—Isaiah 28:17

All men know that they are sinners against God. They also know that, as sinners, they are not safe but are in peril; therefore, they are anxious to find some refuge for safety. They know they might find this to be an obstacle to forsaking sin and turning to the Lord, but they do not choose to forsake their sins. So there seems to be no convenient recourse but to hide themselves under some refuge.

Our text speaks of *"the refuge of lies."* It is obvious that men who resort to lies for a refuge regard those lies not as lies, but as truth. This fact leads us to raise the primary fundamental question, Do we have any rule or standard that will show what is truth and what is falsehood? Men have countless opinions about religion, and not all of them can be true. How, then, can we determine which are true and which are false?

We have an infallible test. Let us examine this test.

Salvation, to be real and available, must be salvation from sin. Everything else fails. Any system of religion that does not break the power of sin is a lie. If it does not expel selfishness and lust for the things of the world, and if it does not generate love for God and man, joy, peace, and all the fruits of the Spirit, it is false and worthless. Any system that fails in this vital respect is a lie, can be of no use, and is no better than a curse.

That which does not generate in us the spirit of heaven and make us like God—no matter where it originates or by what reasoning it is defended—is a lie. If it is fled to as a refuge, then it is a *"refuge of lies."*

Again, if it does not generate a spirit of prayer, does not unify us with God, and does not bring us into fellowship and sympathy with Him, it is a lie.

If it does not produce a heavenly mind, expel a worldly mind, and wean us from the love of the world, it is a lie. If it does not generate in us the love required in the Scriptures, the love of God and of His worship and of His people—indeed, of all mankind—and if it does not produce all the states of mind that equip the soul for heaven, then it utterly fails in its purpose.

Here I must stop a moment to notice an objection. Some people may say, "The Gospel does not, in fact, do for men all that you claim. It does not make professing Christians heavenly minded, dead to the world, full of love, joy, and peace."

Suppose you have a medicine that, when applied to a certain disease, will certainly cure. The medicine has healing power, but it must be *applied*. A man may buy the medicine, find it to be bitter, and store it away in his cupboard and never take it. He may also provide himself with a counterfeit to take in its place, or he may follow it with something that will instantly counteract its influence in the system. In any case, the effectiveness of the medicine is not disproved; he only proves that he has not used it fairly and honestly.

So it is with the Gospel. You must take it and use it according to the directions; otherwise, its failure is not its fault, but yours.

It is to no advantage, then, to say that the Gospel does not save men from sin. It may indeed be counterfeited; it may be rejected; but he who receives it to his heart will surely find his heart blessed by it. The Gospel does transform men from sin to holiness; it makes men peaceful, holy, and heavenly, in life and in death. Millions of such cases can be seen in the record of the world's history. Their lives demonstrate the reality and preciousness of the salvation that the Gospel promises.

Let us now examine some things that lack this decisive characteristic. They do not save the soul from sin; they are refuges of lies.

An Unsanctifying Hope of Heaven

Speaking of what God's children will one day be, John said, *"We know that when He* [Christ] *is revealed, we shall be like Him, for we shall see Him as He is. And everyone who has this hope in Him purifies himself, just as He is pure"* (1 John 3:2–3). A good hope purifies the heart. But certainly there are hopes that fail to purify the hearts of the people who hold them. Those hopes are lies. They cannot possibly be sound and true. On their very face, it stands revealed that they are worthless—a mere *"refuge of lies."* The stronger and more unwavering those hopes are, the more deluding they are. But there is no hope in Christ that does not bring the heart to Christ.

An Old Experience

An old experience that is all old is a lie. There was once an elderly gentleman who had his old religious experience written down and laid away with his deeds for his land, to be kept until his time of need. This being all the evidence he had of his piety, he used to refer to it from time to time for his comfort. When the time came for him to die, he felt the need for this record of his religion, and he asked his daughter to bring it to him. She returned with only the sad story that the mice had found their way to his drawer and had eaten up the paper—the dying man's only evidence of piety! He would now have to die in despair; he had no other hope but this! Such a refuge, dear reader, is only lies.

Self-Righteousness

There are two forms of self-righteousness—the legal and the Gospel—both of which are refuges of lies.

The legal form of self-righteousness depends on the doing of duty, on always trying to work out salvation by deeds of law. The Gospel form sets itself to get grace by works. Men try to get a new heart not by trying to turn from all sin, but by praying for it. A man once told me, "I tried to become religious." When I asked him what he had done in his attempt to become religious, he replied, "I prayed for a new heart." The trouble was that he did not do what God says he must do, and that is to make himself a new heart and a new spirit. (See Ezekiel 18:31.) He did not repent; he did not bow his heart to God. Therefore, all his efforts came short of what God requires. They failed to save his soul from sin.

There is a great deal of this Gospel self-righteousness—this throwing off the responsibility upon God.

Universalism

Universalism is an old *"refuge of lies."* Let me give you an example. Going along the road in my carriage, I was passing by a young man and asked him if he would like a ride. He accepted the offer. Almost immediately he told me he was a Universalist and came out strongly in defense of his system. I said to him, "I am not well and may not live long. I do not dare to be deceived in this matter." He said that he was sure enough of its truth. He had heard many intelligent men say so and prove it from Scripture. I said to him, "I have one objection. If Universalism is true, there are several facts that I cannot account for. One set of facts is that I have known some families—once reputed to be upright, moral, and well respected—to become loose in morals, forsake the house of God, turn to strong drink, and become fearfully cruel. The families undergoing this change almost always become Universalists.

"On the other hand, I have never known a holy, prayerful Universalist to backslide into gospel truth, forsake his Universalism and his morality, and degenerate into vice and true faith simultaneously. I have known men who were reformed from drunkenness and vice, and then became true believers of the Gospel. But I have never known men reform from vice into Universalism. In short, it seems to me that thousands of facts reveal a natural sympathy between vice and Universalism on the one hand, and between virtue and gospel truth on the other."

By this time, he began to feel troubled and said, "I am afraid I am all wrong. Would you believe it? I am running away from being converted. There is a revival in my town, and I am running away from it." "You are," I said. "And do you think it will hurt you? Will it do you any harm?"

He looked deeply anxious and said, "I don't believe Universalism can save me. Everybody knows it never did save anybody and never can."

The same must be said of Unitarianism.* Some who bear this name are not really Unitarians. But wherever you find people who deny depravity, regeneration, and atonement, you will certainly find that their system does not make them heavenly minded, holy, or humble. You do not need to reason with them to find this out; you need only to take the facts of their history.

Universalism never saved any man from sin. Look at the facts! They alone are sufficient to show its utter falsehood. The same is true of Mormonism

---

* Unitarianism denies the Christian doctrine of the Trinity and the Christian doctrine of the deity of Jesus Christ.

and all similar delusions. We do not need to write books against this and similar lies; it is far too obvious that this system saves no man from sin. It is therefore a *"refuge of lies,"* deceiving men into hopes that can never be realized. And so we say of every creed and system that does not save men from sin and prepare them for heaven.

Other Refuges of Lies

And now, I want you to notice what God says. He declares, *"The hail will sweep away the refuge of lies, and the waters will overflow the hiding place."* No doubt this hail is the symbol of God's displeasure. It is fitting that God should be displeased with these refuges of lies. He loves truth too well to have the least sympathy with lies. He loves the souls of men too deeply to have any patience with things so destructive. Therefore, He loathes all these refuges of lies, and He has solemnly declared that the hail will sweep them all away.

Religious Artificiality and Formality

"The waters," He declares, *"will overflow the hiding place."* Every resource that leaves the soul in sin is a hiding place. All religious artificiality is only a hiding place, none better than the other. To put on the mere appearance of devotion and holiness, as if God could be made to believe you are sincere and could not see through it all—this is a flimsy hiding place indeed. The same is true of all religious formality—going through the motions of worship, being in the church, being baptized, and so on. What comes of it all unless a person's piety is filled with life and that life is the soul of real holiness?

The Church

Many people hide in the church. Judas Iscariot crept in there to hide. A minister of the Dutch Reformed Church once told me of a certain case. A man who had been confirmed in that church was out at sea in a fearful storm. It was a time of intense alarm, and many who were with him were exceedingly fearful of death, as well as what lay beyond. When they said to him, "Why are you so calm?" he replied, "What have I to fear? I belong to the South Dutch!"

Orthodox Creeds

Many hide under orthodox creeds. They are not Unitarians; they are not Mormons; they are not Universalists; they are orthodox! They think that religious opinions held so strongly will ensure their safety.

A Sinful Nature

Others hide under the plea of a sinful nature. They say they are naturally unable to do anything. Here they have found a sure retreat. They are very willing to do their duty before God, but this sinful nature is all against them. Thus, what can they do? This is a *"refuge of lies."*

The Shortcomings of Believers

Some people dodge under believers' shortcomings. I fear there are many people like this in the church. But this hiding place will fail you in the day of trial! When the hail comes and the storm arises fearfully, and when the awful thunder breaks with an appalling crash, you will try in vain to find that man whose faults seemed to excuse your own—to hide under his wing! Where is he now? If he is as bad as you claim, how much can he help you in that all-devouring storm? If he is not as good as he should be, you ought to be better than he, and not try to hide yourself under his shortcomings.

REMARKS

1. Sinners know these things to be refuges of lies, because these things do not save men from their sins. Certainly they must see this and know it to be the truth. They resort to these refuges, not as being quite fully true, but as an excuse for delay. What a miserable deception! They are not honest, and therefore they should not think it strange if they are deluded. They admit that if one lives like Christ, all will be well, and they know that nothing less than this will give them safety.

2. Of course, to seek a *"refuge of lies"* is to tempt God to destroy you. How can it be otherwise? Remember the test, a plain and simple principle: only that which saves from sin is true; all else is false and ruinous.

You have some hope of a happy future. What is this hope? Is it good or bad? Is it truthful and sure, or is it a *"refuge of lies"*? Does your hope sanctify you; does it make you humble, holy, prayerful? Does your faith purify your heart? Do you have the fruits of the Spirit—love, joy, peace, long-suffering? (See Galatians 5:22–23.) Do you have daily communion with God? Are you so united to Him that you can say, "Truly I have fellowship with the Father"? (See

1 John 1:3.) If so, this will be a hiding place indeed—not one that the hail will sweep away, but one that will save the soul.

3. Do you have the life of God in your soul? Does it pervade your heart and diffuse itself over all the chambers of your soul? Let nothing less than this satisfy your mind.

Catholics talk about the Virgin and the sacraments and absolution. What are all these things—and a thousand more things like them—good for if they do not save from sin? What is the use of running after these things that do not save?

But you say, "I love to believe that everyone will be saved; it makes me so happy." But does it make you holy? Does it renew your heart? This is the only sure test.

You say, "I do not believe as you do." But here are the facts. You are in sin. Are you saved from your sin by your system? If so, then it is well; if not so, then it is not well. Does believing a lie make it the truth? If you were to believe that you could walk on the water, or that water could not drown you, and you leap overboard, would your belief save you?

Dying sinner, all those refuges of lies will surely deceive and destroy you. It is time for you to arise and say, "I must have the religion of Jesus. Not having it, I cannot go where Jesus is. With a lie in my right hand, what can I hope for?" None of you, I hope, have reached that forlorn state described by the prophet: *"A deceived heart has turned him aside; and he cannot deliver his soul, nor say, 'Is there not a lie in my right hand?'"* (Isa. 44:20).

O sinner, there is a Refuge for you that is not one of lies. There is a Hiding Place for you that no waters can reach to overwhelm. It lies far above their course. Oh, take refuge in Christ! Do away with these refuges of lies! Cry out, "Give me Christ, and none other! Christ and Him only, for what have I to do with lies and delusions?" You need to come into such communion with Christ that His power and presence and fullness will flow through your heart fully and freely, and be in you *a fountain of water springing up into everlasting life*" (John 4:14).

Five

The Wicked Heart
Set to Do Evil

*Because the sentence against an evil work is not
executed speedily, therefore the heart of the sons of men
is fully set in them to do evil.*
—Ecclesiastes 8:11

This Scripture verse evidently assumes that the present world is not a state of rewards and punishments, in which men are treated according to their character and conduct. This fact is not actually affirmed, but it is assumed, both here and throughout the Bible. Everybody knows that ours is not a state of present rewards and punishments; the experience and observation of every man testify to this fact with convincing power. Thus, it is entirely proper that the Bible should assume it to be a known truth. Every man who reads his Bible sees that many things in it are assumed to be true. These are precisely the things that every man knows to be true and that he could not know more certainly if God had affirmed them on every page of the Bible.

In the case of this truth, every man knows that he himself is not punished as he has deserved to be in the present world. He sees the same thing in the case of his neighbors. The psalmist was so astounded by the injustice of things in this world that he was greatly perplexed, *"until,"* he said, *"I went into the sanctuary of God; then I understood their end"* (Ps. 73:17).

It is also assumed in this passage that, by nature, all men have a common heart. One general fact is asserted of them all, and in this way they are assumed to have a common character: *"The heart of the sons of men is fully set in them to do evil."* The Scriptures affirm this elsewhere about mankind: *"The LORD saw that the wickedness of man was great in the earth, and that every intent of the thoughts of his heart was only evil continually"* (Gen. 6:5). This is the common method in which God speaks of sinners in His Word. He always assumes that, by nature, they have the same inclination toward sin.

What Is the Heart?

Our text verse, Ecclesiastes 8:11, also shows the moral nature of the sinner's heart: *"fully set...to do evil."* Let us take a moment to discover what is meant here by the term *"heart."*

It is obvious that this term is used in the Bible to mean various things. Sometimes it denotes the conscience, as in the passage that reads, *"If our heart condemns us, God is greater than our heart"* (1 John 3:20). Sometimes the term is used for the reason, the mind. But here it is most evidently used to denote the will, because this is the only power of the mind that can be said to be *set*—determined upon a given course of voluntary action. The will is the faculty that sets itself upon a chosen course;

therefore, in our text, the term *heart* must mean "the will." Otherwise, no sense can be made of the passage.

But in what direction and to what end are the wills of wicked men fully set? They are set to do evil. God's Word solemnly affirms this fact.

In order to explain this verse further, let me say that it does not imply that men do evil for the sake of the evil itself. It does not imply that sinning, considered as disobedience to God, is their direct objective. Indeed, the drunkard does not drink *because* it is wicked to drink, but he drinks *despite* its wickedness. He drinks for the present good it promises, not for the sake of sinning.

The same is true of the man who tells lies. His goal is not to break God's law, but to get something good for himself by lying; yet he tells the lie despite God's prohibition. His heart may become fully set upon the practice of lying whenever it is convenient for him and he thinks he may gain some good by it. God's efforts to dissuade him from his course are thereby made futile.

The same is true of stealing, adultery, and other sins. We are not to suppose that men set their hearts upon these sins out of love for pure wickedness. Rather, they do so for the sake of the good they hope to gain thereby. The licentious man would perhaps be glad if it were not wicked to gratify his passion; but though it is wicked, he sets his heart to do it. Adam and Eve ate the forbidden fruit. Why? Because they saw it was beautiful, and they were told it would make them wise. Hence, they took and ate for the good they hoped to gain—in spite of God's prohibition.

It is sometimes said that sinners love sin for its own sake—out of a pure love of sin *as* sin, simply because it is disobedience to God—with a natural relish, just as wolves love flesh. But this is not true—certainly not in many cases. The simple truth is, men do not set their hearts upon the sin for its own sake, but upon sinning for the sake of the good they hope to get from it.

The Power of Selfishness

Take a closer look at the language used in the text verse: *"the heart...fully set...to do evil."* One man is greedy; he wants to get money by fair means, if possible, but he will be sure to find a way to get it. Another man is ambitious. The love of fame and reputation fills and fires his soul. He may become very polite and very amiable in his manners—sometimes even very religious, if religion is popular. But he is altogether selfish, and he is no less selfish for being so very religious.

Selfishness takes on a thousand forms, but each form is sinful, for the whole mind should give itself up to serve God and to perform every duty as revealed to one's mind. What did Eve do? She gave herself up to gratify her thirst for knowledge and for self-indulgence. She agreed to believe the lying spirit who told her it was *"a tree desirable to make one wise"* (Gen. 3:6). She thought this tree must be very important. It was also, apparently, good for food, and her appetite was whetted. The more she looked, the more interested she became; and now what should she do? God had forbidden her to touch it. Should she obey God or her own excited appetite? Despite

God's command, she ate the fruit. Was that a sin? Many would think it was a very small sin. But it was real rebellion against God, and He could not do anything but avenge it with His terrific displeasure.

It is the same everywhere. To yield to the demands of appetite and passion, against God's claims, is to commit a grave sin. All men are required to fear and obey God, however much self-denial and sacrifice it may cost.

I said that selfishness often assumes a religious exterior. At the outset, the mind may be powerfully affected by some of the great and stirring truths of the Gospel, but then it takes on an entirely selfish view, caring only to escape punishment and to make religion a matter of gain. In such cases, the mind utterly misunderstands the intentions of the Gospel, losing sight of the great fact that it seeks to eradicate man's selfishness and draw his heart into pure benevolence. Making this radical mistake, the mind sees the whole Gospel system as a scheme for indulging in sin. Let me give you an example.

A certain individual supposes that Christ's righteousness, having been imputed to him, allows him to go on living in sin. That is, he supposes that he is entirely exempt from the penalty of violating the law. He even thinks that he has the honors and rewards of full obedience while he still has all the self-indulgences of a life of sin. Horrible!

Examine such a case thoroughly, and you will see that selfishness is at the bottom of all the religion in it. The man was worldly before and is devout now, but he is devout for the same reason that he was worldly. His selfish heart is the basis for each system. He seeks the same ends in the same spirit;

his moral character remains unchanged. He may pray, but if he does, he asks God to do some great things for him, to promote his own selfish purposes. He does not have the faintest idea of committing himself to God's interests in such a way that he will be in perfect harmony with God, desiring and seeking only God's interests, and having no interests other than God's to serve at all.

To illustrate this point, let us suppose that a parent should say to his children, "I will give you my property if you will work with me and truly identify your interests with mine. If you are not willing to do this, I will disinherit you." Some of the children may take a perfectly selfish view of this offer and may say to themselves, "I will do just enough for Father to get his money. I will make him think that I am very zealous for his interests, and I will do just enough to secure the offered rewards. Why should I do any more?"

Or suppose there is a human government that offers rewards to offenders if they will return to obedience. The real spirit of the offer asks the criminals to be sincerely devoted in their hearts to the best good of the government. But the criminals may take a wholly selfish view of the case; they may decide to accept the proposal just enough to secure the rewards, and only for the sake of the rewards.

The Ruler of the universe wants and expects the actual devotion of people's hearts, their real goodwill. If they would give Him this much, He would reward them abundantly. But how can He be satisfied with them if they are altogether selfish?

A man may be as selfish in praying as he is in stealing. He may even be far more wicked, for he may more seriously mock God and more impiously attempt to bribe the Almighty to promote his own selfish purposes. As if he supposed he could make the Searcher of hearts his own instrument, he may insolently try to persuade Him to play into his hands. Thus he may most grievously tempt God to His face.

The Sinner's Depravity

The text verse affirms that *"the heart...of men is fully set in them to do evil."* Perhaps some of you think otherwise; you don't believe in such depravity. A mother may say, "I think my daughter is receptive toward religion. Do you think she is converted?" No, I do not think she is converted, but I think she is receptive toward religion. Does she satisfy the claims of God by being a friend of His government and His reputation? I cannot give you an answer about that. Ask her to repent, and what does she say? She will tell you she cannot.

How striking the fact that you may go through the ranks of society, and you will find this position almost everywhere. The sinner says, "I cannot repent; I cannot believe." What is the matter? Where is the trouble?

Go to that daughter, thought to be so receptive toward religion. She is so amiable and gentle that she cannot bear to see any pain inflicted on any creature. But when you present to her the claims of God, what does she say? "I cannot; I cannot obey God. I cannot repent of my sin," she says. But what does it entail to repent, that this amiable young lady, so friendly toward religion, should be incapable of repenting? What is the matter? Is God so unreasonable in His demands that He imposes upon you things quite impossible for you to do? Or is it that you have no regard for His feelings and are so reckless of the truth that, for the sake of self-justification, you will charge Him with the most flagrant injustice, falsely implying that the wrong is all on His side and none on yours? Is this a very amiable character trait in you? Is this one of your proofs that the human heart is not fully set to do evil?

You say you cannot repent and love God. You find it quite impossible to make up your mind to serve and please God. What is the matter? Are there no sufficient reasons apparent to your mind why you should give up your heart to God? No reasons? Heaven, earth, and hell may all combine to pour upon you their reasons for fearing and loving God, and yet you cannot! Why? Because your heart is fully set within you to do evil rather than good. You are altogether committed to the pleasing of self. Jesus may plead with you; your friends may plead; heaven and hell may lift up their united voices to plead; and every reason that can press on your heart—whether from your conscience, hope and fear, angels and devils, God or man—may pass before your mind. But, alas! Your heart is so fully set to do evil that nothing can change you. What is this *cannot?* Nothing less or more than a vehement *will not!*

A good-natured lady will insist that she is not much depraved. Oh, no, not she. She will not steal! True, her selfishness has a most tender and delicate appearance. She cannot bear to see a kitten in distress, but what does she care for God's rights or feelings? What does she care for the rights of Jesus

Christ? What does she care for the feelings and sympathies of the crucified Son of God? Just nothing at all. What, then, is all her tender sensitivity worth? Doves and kittens have even more of this than she. She undoubtedly has many tender ties, but they are all under the control of a perfectly selfish heart.

Eve, too, was amiable. Indeed, she was a truly pious woman before she sinned, and Adam no doubt thought she could be trusted in all things. But notice how terribly she fell! And all the sons and daughters of her race have fallen with her. Giving up their hearts to a refined selfishness, they reject God's most righteous claims, and they are fallen!

If you were to go through all the ranks of society, you would see the same thing. Go to the pirate ship, with the captain armed to the teeth and the fire of hell in his eye. Ask him to receive an offered Savior and repent of his sins, and he will give you the very same answer as that amiable daughter does—he cannot repent. His heart, too, is so fully set within him to do evil that he cannot get his own consent to turn from his sins to God.

Oh, this horrible commitment of the heart to do evil! It is the only reason why the Holy Spirit is needed to change the sinner's heart. Except for this, you would no more need the Holy Spirit than an angel of light does. How fearfully strong is the sinner's heart against God! He seems to have almost an omnipotence of strength to oppose and resist the claims of God! The motives of truth may be as high as a mountain and may beat upon his iron heart, yet he braces up his nerves to withstand God. Is there anything that he will not resist sooner than submit his will to God?

107

The Sentence upon Sinners

Our text verse also assumes, but does not affirm, that sinners are already under sentence. The verse says, *"Because the sentence...is not executed speedily,"* implying that the sentence has already been passed and only awaits the appointed time when it will be carried out. If you have ever attended a court of justice, you know that the sentencing comes after trial and conviction. Just before the sentence is given, the room is as still as death. The judge rises, reviews the case, and comes to the solemn conclusion: you are convicted by this court of the crime alleged, and now you are to receive your sentence. The sentence is then pronounced.

After this solemn transaction, execution is commonly deferred for a period of time. The purpose of this waiting period may be either to give the criminal opportunity to secure a pardon, or if there is no hope of this, at least to give him some days or weeks for serious reflection in which he may secure the peace of his soul with God. But after the sentence is given, the case is fully decided. No further doubt of the criminal's guilt can intervene to affect the case; the possibility of pardon is the only remaining hope. The awful sentence seals his doom—unless it is possible that pardon may be had.

That sentence—how it sinks into the heart of the guilty culprit! "You are now," says the judge, "ordered back to the place from which you came, to be kept in fetters, under close confinement, until the day appointed. Then you will be taken from your prison between the hours of ten and twelve, as the case may be, and hung by the neck until you are dead. And may God have mercy on your soul!" The sentence has been passed; the court has done its work; it only remains for the sheriff to do his as the executioner of justice, and the fearful scene closes.

The Bible represents the similar case of the sinner. He is under sentence, but his sentence is not executed speedily. Some delay in punishment is allowed. The arrangements of the divine government require no court, no jury. The law itself says, *"The soul who sins shall die"* (Ezek. 18:20), and *"Cursed is everyone who does not continue in all things which are written in the book of the law, to do them"* (Gal. 3:10). Thus, the mandate of the law involves the sentence on every sinner—a sentence from which there can be no escape and no reprieve except by a pardon. What a position this is for the sinner!

But consider another strange fact. Because sentence is not executed speedily; because there is some delay in carrying it out; because Mercy prevails to secure for the condemned culprit a few days' delay, so that punishment will not tread close on the heels of crime, *"therefore the heart of the sons of men is fully set in them to do evil."* How astounding! What a perversion and abuse of the gracious design of the King in granting a little respite from instant execution!

Let us see how it would look in the case of a friend. He has committed a fearful crime, is arrested, put on trial, convicted, sentenced, and handed over to the sheriff to await the day and hour of his execution. The judge says to him, "I defer the execution, so that you may have opportunity to secure a pardon from the governor. I assure you that the governor is a most compassionate man. He loves to grant pardons;

he has already pardoned thousands. If you will give up your spirit of rebellion, he will most freely forgive you. I beg of you, therefore, that you will do no such thing as attempt a justification of your crime. Don't think of escaping death except by casting yourself upon his mercy. Don't flatter yourself that there can be any other refuge."

Now suppose this friend begins, "I have done nothing—nothing at all. I am simply a martyr to truth and justice! I have done nothing very bad—nothing that any government ought to notice. I don't believe I will be sentenced. I will live as long as the best of you." So the man makes excuses, though he is already condemned. He acts as if he is preparing for a trial, as if he expects to prove his innocence before the court. Perhaps he even sets himself to oppose and curse the government, railing at its laws and at its officers, deeming nothing too bad to say of them, indulging himself in the most outrageous opposition, abusing the very men whose mercy has spared his forfeited life. Anyone would be shocked to see such a case—to see a man ignoring all propriety, cursing the government whose righteous laws he had just broken and then whose mercy he had most flagrantly abused! Yet our text affirms this to be the case of the sinner, and all observation supports it. You have seen it over ten thousand times; you can look back and see it in your own case. You know it is all true—fearfully, terribly true.

If today it were revealed to you in some striking, awful manner that your soul is damned, you would be thunderstruck. You do not believe the simple declaration of Jehovah as it stands recorded on the pages of the Bible. You are continually saying to yourself, "I will not be condemned in the end. I will just keep going along. I will still dare to tempt God's patience. I do not at all believe that He will send me to hell. At least I will go on one more season, and if after that I find it quite advisable to turn, I will do so. But at the present time, why should I fear to set my heart fully in the way God has forbidden?"

Where will you find a parallel to such wickedness? You need only look so far as a state of moral audacity that can abuse God's richest mercies, that can coolly say, "God is so good that I will abuse Him all I can. God loves me so much that I will go on insulting Him and perverting His long-suffering to the utmost hardening of my soul in sin and rebellion."

Let each sinner be assured that the day of execution is truly set. God will not pass over it. When it arrives, there can be no more delay. God does not wait because He is in doubt about the justice of the sentence or because His heart questions Him in view of its terrible execution. He only waits so that He may try to persuade you to embrace mercy. This is all; this is the only reason why judgment has lingered for a long time and the sword of justice has not long since struck you down.

Here is another interesting fact. God has not only deferred execution, but at immense cost He has provided means for the safe exercise of mercy. You know it is naturally a dangerous thing to bestow mercy—there is so much danger of it weakening the force of the law and encouraging men to trample it down in hope of becoming exempt from its statutes. But God has provided a glorious testimony in favor of the law, showing that it is in His heart to sustain it at every sacrifice. He could not forgive sin until, before the entire universe, His injured and insulted law was honored. Having done all this in the sacrifice of His own Son on Calvary, He can forgive without fear of consequences—as long as each candidate for pardon will first be penitent.

Therefore, God's heart of mercy is opened wide and no fear of evil consequences from unearned pardons disturbs the exercise of that mercy. Before atonement, justice stood with brandished sword, demanding vengeance on the guilty. But through Christ's atoning blood, God rescued His law from peril. He lifted it up from beneath the impious foot of the transgressor, set it on high in safety and glory, and now opens wide the blessed door of mercy. Now He comes in the person of His Spirit and invites you in. He comes to your heart, sinner, to offer you the freest possible pardon for all your sin. Do you hear that gentle rap at your door? *"Behold, I stand at the door and knock. If anyone hears My voice and opens the door, I will come in to him and dine with him, and he with Me"* (Rev. 3:20).

Look at Jesus' hands. Have they not been pierced? Do you know those hands? Do you know where they have been to be nailed through and through? See those locks of hair, wet with dew. How long have they been kept outside, waiting for the door to open? (See Song of Solomon 5:2–3.) Who is it that comes? Is it the sheriff of justice? Has he come with his armed men to drag you away to execution? Oh, no; but One comes with the cup of mercy in His hands. He approaches your prison gate, His eyes wet with the tears of compassion, and extends that cup of mercy to your parched lips. Do you see that face— marred more than any man's (Isa. 52:14)—and yet you are only more fully set to do evil? Is this the state of your heart toward the God of mercy? Where can we find an equivalent to such guilt? Can it be found anywhere else in the universe but in this crazy world?

Heaven must be wonderfully interested in the scenes and transactions of earth. Angels desire to look into these things. (See 1 Peter 1:12.) Oh, how the whole universe looks on with inquisitive wonder to see what Christ has done, and to see how the sinners for whom He has suffered and done all repay His amazing love! When they see you set your heart more fully upon doing evil, they stand back aghast at such unparalleled wickedness! What can be done for such sinners but to leave them to the madness and doom of their choice? God has no other alternative. If you will abuse Him, He must execute His law and its fearful sentence of eternal death.

Suppose it were a human government and a similar state of facts were to occur. Is it not obvious that this government might as well relinquish its power at once as refrain from punishing the crime? The same is true of God. Although He has no pleasure in the sinner's death (Ezek. 33:11), and although He will never slay you because He delights in it, how can He do anything other than carry out His law if He wishes to sustain it? How could He excuse Himself for any failure in sustaining it? Will you stand out against Him and flatter yourself that He will not execute His awful sentence upon you? Oh, sinner, there is no possibility that you can pass the appointed time without execution. Human laws may possibly fail to be carried out, but God's laws can never fail! God, through the apostle Peter, said, *"For a long time their judgment has not been idle, and their destruction does not slumber"* (2 Pet. 2:3).

REMARKS

1. Let me ask those of you who profess faith, Do you think you believe these truths? Suppose you are the parent of a child whom you know to be under sentence of death. However, until today, you have not known exactly when he will be executed. Now you discover that this is the very day and hour set for his execution. How do you feel? Would not the knowledge of such facts disturb you?

You know that an eternal death in hell must be far more awful than any public execution on earth. If your own son were under sentence for execution on earth, how would you feel? If you believe him to be under the far more awful sentence of hell, how, in fact, *do* you feel?

But let us extend this case a little. Years ago your son went to sea. For a long time, you have not seen him or even heard a word from him. How often your troubled mind has dwelt on his case! You do not know how he is doing, but you fear the worst. You had reason to think that his principles were not firm when he left home, and you are afraid he has fallen into worse and still worse society, until it may be that he has become a bold transgressor. As you are talking these things over with your wife and searching for any clue you might find as to your son's whereabouts, all at once the doorbell rings. A messenger comes in and hands you a letter. You take it, open it, read a few words, and suddenly fall back in your seat. The letter drops from your hand—oh, you can't read it!

Your wife wonders what has happened and inquires of you. She rushes forward and seizes the fallen letter; she reads a few words, and her heart breaks with agony. What's the matter? Your son has been sentenced to die, and he has sent word to see if his father and mother can come and see him before he dies. In early morning you are off. You hurry to the prison and learn the details of the painful case. You see at a glance that there can be no hope of release unless your son is pardoned. The governor lives nearby, so you rush to his house; however, you find him to be stern and inexorable.

With palpitating hearts and a load on your aching souls, you plead and plead, but all seems to be in vain. He says, "Your son has been so wicked and has committed such crimes, he must be hung. The good of the nation demands it, and I cannot allow my sympathies to overrule my sense of justice and my convictions of the public good." But you, the agonized parents, must hold on. Oh, what a conflict in your minds! How the case burns upon your hearts! At last the boy's mother breaks out, "Sir, are you a father? Do you have a son?" "Yes, one son," he replies. "Where is he?" "Gone to California." "How long has it been since you heard from him? Suppose he, too, should fall! Suppose you were to feel such grief as ours, and have to mourn over a fallen son!"

The governor now sees himself as a father. All the latent sensitivity of the father's heart is aroused within him. Calling to his private secretary, he says,

"Make out a pardon for their son!" What a flood of emotions you then pour out!

All this is very natural. No man deems this strange at all.

But now examine the case of the sinner, condemned to an eternal hell. If your spiritual ears were opened, you would hear the chariot wheels rolling—the great Judge coming in His chariot of thunder. You would see the sword of Death gleaming in the air and ready to strike down the hardened sinner. But take the case of a supposedly Christian father praying for his ungodly son. He thinks he *ought* to pray for him once or twice a day, so he begins. But soon he has almost forgotten his subject. He hardly knows or thinks what he is praying about. God says, "Pray for your dying son! Lift up your cries for him while mercy yet lingers and pardon can be found." But where are the Christian parents who pray for a sentenced and soon-to-be-executed son? They say they believe the Bible, but *do they?* Do they *act* as if they believe even half of its awful truths about sentenced sinners ready to go down to an eternal hell?

What is wrong with the so-called believer who has no spirit of prayer and no power with God? He is an infidel! When God says a son is sentenced to die, when the angel of death may come in one hour to cut him down in his guilt and sin and to send his spirit quickly to hell, and yet the father or the mother have no feeling in the case, then they are infidels; they do not believe what God has said.

2. Let me make another supposition. Suppose you are one of the afflicted parents who has gone to the governor. You have poured out your griefs before him and have at last wrenched a pardon from his

stern hands. You rush from his house toward the prison, so delighted that you scarcely touch the ground. Coming near, you hear songs of merriment, and you say, "How our son must be agonized with unsuitable and unpleasant company!" You then meet the sheriff. "Who," you ask, "can sing so merrily in a prison?" "It is your own son," replies the sheriff. "He has no idea that he will be executed. In fact, he swears he will burn down the governor's house; indeed, he manifests a most determined spirit, as if his heart were fully set on evil." This is distressing news, you think, but you are sure you can subdue his wicked and proud heart. "We will show him the pardon and tell him how the governor feels. We are sure this will subdue him. He cannot withstand such kindness and compassion."

You go to the prison door; you gain admittance and show your son the pardon. You tell him how much time and effort it has cost you and how tenderly the governor feels in the case. But he takes it from you, tears it to pieces, and tramples it under his feet! "You must be deranged!" you say to him. But suppose it is only depravity of the heart, and you know that such must be the case. "Oh," you cry out, "this is worst of all! Our son is not willing to be pardoned—not willing to be saved! This is worse than all the rest. Well, we must go to our desolate home. We are done with our son! We acquired a pardon for him with our tears, but he will not accept it. There is nothing more that we can do."

You turn sadly away, not caring even to say goodbye. You go home doubly saddened—that he should deserve to die both for his original crimes, and also for his yet greater crime of refusing the offered pardon.

117

The day of execution comes; the sheriff is there to do his duty. He takes his culprit from the prison to the place of execution. The multitude gathers around and follows sadly along. Suddenly a messenger rushes up to say to the criminal, "You have torn to pieces one pardon, but here is yet one more. Will you have this?" With proud disdain, he spurns even this last offer of pardon! Now where are the sympathies of all the land? Does anyone say, "How cruel to hang a young man, and for only such a crime?" No; no one is saying any such thing. They see the need for law and justice; they know that law so outraged must be allowed to vindicate itself in the culprit's execution. Now the sheriff proclaims, "Just fifteen minutes to live," and even these minutes he spends abusing the governor and insulting the majesty of the law.

The dreadful hour arrives, and at the last moment he trembles under the grasp of death. Then all is still forever! He is gone, and Law itself has been sustained in the fearful execution of its sentence. All the people feel that this is righteous. They cannot possibly think otherwise. Even his parents have no word of complaint to utter. They approve the governor's course; they endorse the sentence. They say, "We did think he would accept the pardon; but since he would not, let him be accursed! We love good government; we love the blessings of law and order in society more than we love iniquity and crime. He was indeed our son, but he was also the son of the Devil!"

But let us attend the execution of some of the sinners from our own congregations. You are brought out for your execution. We see the messenger; we hear the sentence read—we see that your fatal hour has come. Shall we turn and curse God? No, we will do no such thing. When your day of execution arrives; when you gasp, gasp, and die; when your guilty, terror-stricken soul goes wailing down the sides of the pit, will we go away complaining about God and His justice? No! Why not? Because you might have had mercy, but you would not take it. Because God waited for you for a long time, but your heart only became more fully set to do evil. All the creatures of the universe look on and see the facts in your case, and with one voice that rings through the vast arch of heaven, they cry, "Just and righteous are You in all Your ways, most holy Lord God!"

Who says this is cruel? What! Should the universe take up arms against Jehovah? No. When the entire universe gathers together around the Great White Throne; when the dreadful sentence goes forth, saying, *"Depart from Me, you cursed"* (Matt. 25:41); and when all the beings move away in dense and vast masses—down, down, they sink to the depths of their dark home. But the saints, with firm step and solemn heart, proclaim that God's law is vindicated. The insulted majesty of both Law and Mercy is now upheld in honor, and all is right.

Heaven is solemn but joyful; the saints are solemn, yet they cannot help rejoicing in their own glorious Father. See the crowds and masses as they move up to heaven. They look back over the plains of burning Sodom and see the smoke ascending up like the smoke of a great furnace. But they pronounce it just, and they do not have one word of complaint to utter.

To the yet living sinner, I tell you that the hour of your execution has not yet arrived. Once more the bleeding hand offers Mercy's cup to your lips. Think a moment; your Savior now offers you mercy. Come; come now and accept it.

What will you say? "I'll still go on in my sins"? Again, all I can say is that the soul of divine love is deeply moved for you. God has done all that He wisely can do to save you. God's people have felt a deep and agonizing interest in you and are ready now to cry, "How can we give him up?" But what more can we do—what more can even God do? With bleeding heart and quivering lip, Mercy has followed you. Jesus Himself said, *"'O Jerusalem, Jerusalem, ...how often I wanted to gather your children together,...but you were not willing!'* (Matt. 23:37). How often I would have saved you, but you were not willing!" Will Jesus look upon you, weep over you, and say, "Oh, that you had known—but now it is hidden from your eyes"?

O dying sinner, what will you say? Shouldn't your response be, "I have wickedly tossed aside salvation's cup long enough. You do not need to say another word. Oh, that bleeding hand! Those weeping eyes! Is it possible that I have withstood a Savior's love so long? I am ready to beg for mercy now, and I rejoice to hear that our God has a father's heart"?

He knows that you have sinned greatly and grievously, but He says, "My compassions have been bleeding and gushing forth toward you these many days. Will you accept at once the terms of mercy and come to Jesus?" What do you say?

Suppose an angel comes down, in robes so pure and so white, unrolls his papers, and produces a pardon in your name, sealed with Jesus' own blood. He opens the Sacred Book, reads the very passage that reveals the love of God, and asks you if you will believe and embrace it. What would you do?

And what should I say to my Lord and Master? When I come to report the matter, must I say that you would not listen? When Christ comes so near to you, and would gladly draw you close to His warm heart, what will you do? Will you still repeat the fatal choice, to spurn His love and dare His injured justice?

Six

Moral Insanity

The heart of the sons of men is full of evil,
and madness is in their heart while they live.
—Ecclesiastes 9:3 KJV

The Bible often ascribes to unconverted men one common heart or disposition. It always divides mankind into two classes, and only two—saints and sinners. The saints have been converted from their sin and have become God's real friends; the others, the sinners, remain His unconverted enemies. According to the Bible, therefore, the heart, in all unrenewed men, is the same in its general character.

In the days of Noah, God *"saw that the wickedness of man was great in the earth, and that every intent of the thoughts of his heart was only evil continually"* (Gen. 6:5). Notice that He was speaking of the thoughts of man's *"heart,"* as if all human beings had one common heart, all alike in moral character. God also testifies through Paul that *"the carnal mind is enmity against God"* (Rom. 8:7). He was not talking about just one man, or a few men, but all men who are of a carnal mind. In our text verse, the phraseology is very expressive: *"the heart of the sons of men is full of evil"*—as if the sons of men had only one heart, all in common, and this one heart were *"full of evil."*

The Madness in Man's Heart

You will notice that this affirmation is not made of one or two men, nor of some men, but of *"the sons of men"*—in other words, of them all. But what is intended by affirming that *"madness is in their heart while they live"*? This is not the madness of anger, but of insanity. True, sometimes people are mad with anger, but this is not the sense of our text. The Bible, as well as customary speech, uses the term *madness* to express insanity. So we understand this to be its sense here.

Insanity is of two kinds. One is of the head, the other of the heart. In the former, the intellect is disordered; in the latter, the will and voluntary powers are disordered. Intellectual insanity destroys one's capacity to act upon moral considerations. The man who is intellectually insane is not, for the time being, a moral agent; moral responsibility is suspended because he cannot *know* his duty and cannot choose responsibly either to do it or not do it. True, when a man makes himself temporarily insane, as by drunkenness, the courts are obliged to hold him responsible for what he does in that state. But the man's guilt is really associated with the voluntary act that created his insanity. A man who gets intoxicated by drinking what he knows is intoxicating, must be held responsible for his acts during his ensuing drunkenness. The reason of this is that he can foresee the danger and can easily avoid it.

The general law is that, while the intellect retains its usual power, moral obligation remains unimpaired.

Moral insanity, on the other hand, is madness of the will. The man retains his intellectual powers unimpaired, but he fully sets his heart upon doing evil. He refuses to yield to the demands of his conscience. He practically discards the obligations of moral responsibility. He has the powers of free moral agency but persistently abuses them. He has a reason that affirms obligation, but he refuses to obey its affirmations. In this form of insanity, the reason remains unimpaired, but the heart deliberately disobeys.

The insanity spoken of in our text verse is moral—that of the heart. By the term *heart,* I mean the will, the voluntary power. The man is intellectually sane, yet he acts as if he were insane.

Manifestations of This Insanity

It is important to point out some of the manifestations of this state of mind. Since the Bible affirms that sinners are mad in their heart, we may naturally expect to see some manifestations of this madness. It is often striking to see how perfectly the Bible portrays human character. Has it done so in reference to this point? Let us see.

Fiction Is Treated like Reality

Who are the morally insane? They are those who, not being intellectually insane, still *act* as if they were. For example, those who are intellectually insane treat fiction as if it were reality, and reality as if it were fiction. They act as if truth were not truth, and as if falsehood were truth. Everyone knows that insane people actually follow the wild dreams of their own imagination, as if those dreams were the sternest reality, and can scarcely be made to feel the force of anything truly real.

In a similar fashion, sinners treat the realities of the spiritual world as if they were not real. Instead, they follow the emptiest phantoms of this world, as if they were stern realities.

Self Is Supreme

Those who are morally insane also act as if self were of supreme importance, and everything else of relatively no importance. Suppose you were to see a man acting this out in common life. He goes around, day after day, assuming that he is the Supreme God, and practically insisting that everybody ought to have a supreme regard to *his* rights, and comparatively little or no regard for other people's rights. Now, if you were to see a man saying this and acting it out, would you not consider him either a blasphemer or insane?

The fact is that while wicked men will try to tell you that they know better, they will act as if all this were true—as if they supposed their own self-interest to be more important than everything else in the universe, and that God's interests and even His rights are nothing in comparison. Every sinner does this. It is an essential element in all sin. Selfish men never regard the rights of anybody else, unless they are in some way linked with their own.

If wicked men really believed their own rights and interests to be supreme in the universe, it would prove them to be intellectually insane, and we would rush to shut them up in the nearest asylum. But when they tell you that they know better, yet they act on this groundless assumption in the face of their better knowledge, we say, with the Bible, that *"madness is in their heart while they live."*

A Focus on the Things of This World

This madness is also manifested in man's relative estimate of time and eternity. His whole life declares that, in his view, it is far more important to secure the good of time than the good of eternity. Yet if a man were to argue this point and were to earnestly assert it, you would know him to be insane and would help him to the madhouse. But suppose he does not *say* this—he dares not say it, for he knows it is not true—yet constantly acts it out and lives on the assumption of its truth. What then? Simply this—he is morally mad. Madness is in his heart.

Now, this is precisely the practice of every one of you who is living in sin. You give preference to time over eternity. You practically say, "Give me the joys of time. Why should I trouble myself yet about the trivial matters of eternity?"

In the same spirit, you assume that the body is more than the soul. But if a man were to affirm this and go around trying to prove it, you would know him to be insane. If he were a friend of yours, your heart would break for his sad misfortune—his powers of reason would be all lost! But if he knows better, yet he practically lives as if it were so, you say, "He is morally insane."

Suppose you see a man destroying his own property, not by accident or mistake, but deliberately. He also injures his own health, as if he has no care for his own interests. You might bring his case before a judge and charge the man with lunacy. The man's goods would then be taken out of his own control, and he would no longer be allowed to squander them. Yet in spiritual things, wicked men deliberately act against their own dearest interests. Though they know how to get wisdom, they will not get it. Having the treasures of heaven placed within their reach, they do not try to secure them. With an infinite wealth of blessedness offered for the mere acceptance, they will not take it as a gift. It is plain that, if men were to act in temporal things as they do in spiritual, they would all be pronounced insane. Any man would swear to it. He would say, "Look, the man acts against his own interests in everything! Who can deny that he is insane? Certainly sane men never do this!"

But in moral questions, wicked men seem to take the utmost pains to subvert their own interests and make themselves destitute forever! Oh, how they impoverish their souls, when they might have the riches of heaven!

Attempts to Bring about the Impossible

Again, those who are morally insane endeavor to bring obvious impossibilities to fruition. For example, they try to make themselves happy in their sins and their selfishness. Yet they know they cannot do it. Ask them, and they will admit the thing is utterly impossible. Yet, despite this conviction, they perpetually try—as if they expect to eventually make the impossibility a possibility.

Now, in moral things, it may not strike you as especially strange, for it is exceedingly common. But suppose you were to see a man doing the same sort of thing in matters of the world. What would you think of him? For example, you see him working hard to build a very long ladder, and you ask him what it is for. He says, "I am going to scale the moon." You see him expending his labor and his money, with the toil of a lifetime, to build a huge ladder with which to scale the moon! Would you not say, "He is certainly insane"? For if he were not really insane, he would know it to be an utter impossibility.

But in spiritual things, men are always trying to bring about a result at least equally impossible—that of being happy in sin. They try to be happy with a mutiny within themselves, with the heart at war against reason and conscience. The pursuit of happiness in sin is as if a man were seeking to bless himself by mangling his own flesh, digging out his own eyes, knocking in his own teeth. Yet as much as men know that they cannot ensure health and comfort by mutilating their own flesh and tearing their own nerves asunder, they know that they cannot obtain happiness in sin and selfishness. Thus, madly doing what they know will always defeat and never ensure real happiness, they prove themselves to be morally insane.

Loss of Confidence in God

Another manifestation of intellectual insanity is loss of confidence in one's best friends. Often this is one of the first and most painful evidences of insanity—the poor man will begin to believe that his dearest friends are determined to ruin him. By no amount of evidence can he be persuaded to think they are his real friends.

In their madness, sinners treat God the same way. While they inwardly know that He is their real friend, they practically treat Him as their worst enemy. Nothing can persuade them to confide in Him as their friend. In fact, they treat Him as if He were the greatest liar in the universe. Amazingly, they practically reverse the regard due respectively to God and to Satan—treating Satan as if he were God, and God as if He were Satan. They believe and obey Satan; they disown, dishonor, and disobey God. How strangely they are willing to reverse the order of things! They would gladly enthrone Satan over the universe, giving him the highest seat in heaven; the almighty and holy God they would send to hell. They do not hesitate to surrender to Satan the place of power over their own hearts that is due to God alone.

I have already pointed out the fact that insane people treat their best friends as if they were their worst enemies, and that this is often the first proof of insanity. If a husband is insane, he will believe that his dear wife is trying to poison him. The first case of real insanity I ever saw made a strong impression on my mind. I was riding on horseback and, coming near a house, I noticed a bedroom window and heard a most unearthly cry coming from it. As soon as I came near enough to catch the words, I heard a most wild, imploring voice saying, "Stranger, stranger, come here—here is the great whore of Babylon. They are trying to kill me; they will kill me." I dismounted, went up to the house, and there found a man shut up in a cage and shouting most bitterly about his wife. As I turned toward her, I saw that she looked sad, as if a load of grief lay heavy on her heart. A tear trembled in her eye. Alas, her dear husband was a maniac! Then I first learned how the insane are likely to regard their best friends.

Now, sinners know better of God and of their other real friends, yet they very commonly treat them in precisely this way. It is just as if they were to go into public places, lift up their voices, and say to all the bystanders, "The Great God is an almighty tyrant! He is not fit to be trusted or loved!"

Sinners know they treat God this way by their actions. They regard religion as if it were inconsistent with their real and highest happiness. I have often met sinners who seemed to think that every attempt to make them Christians is a scheme to take them in and sell them into slavery. They by no means see religion as coming forth from a God of love. Essentially, they treat religion as if embracing it would be their ruin. Yet in all this, they act utterly against their own convictions. They know better. If they did not, their guilt would be exceedingly small compared with what it is.

Apathy toward Important Matters

Another remarkable manifestation of moral insanity is to be greatly excited about insignificant matters and apathetic about the most important matters in the universe. Suppose you see a man excited about straws and pebbles—taking unwearied pains to gather them into heaps and store them away as treasures. Yet when a fire breaks out around his dwelling and the village is in flames, he takes no notice of it and feels no interest. Or suppose people are dying of the plague left and right, but he pays no attention. Would you not say that he must be insane?

This is precisely true of sinners. They are almost infinitely excited about worldly things—straws and pebbles—compared with the treasures that God has offered. But how apathetic they are about the most momentous events in the universe! The vast concerns of their souls scarcely stir up one earnest thought. If they did not know better, you would say, "Certainly their reason is gone." But since they do know better, you cannot say less than that they are morally insane, that *"madness is in their heart while they live."*

The conduct of impenitent men is the epitome of irrationality. When you see it as it is, you will get a more vivid idea of irrationality than you can get from any other source. You see this in the ends to which they devote themselves, and in the means that they employ to secure them. All is utterly unreasonable. An end madly chosen and sought by means madly devised—this is the life history of the masses who reject God. If this were also the result of wrong intellectual judgments, we would say at once that the entire race has gone mad.

Bedlam itself offers no higher evidence of intellectual insanity than every sinner does of moral insanity. You may go and visit every room occupied by the inmates of a lunatic asylum; you will not find one insane person who gives higher evidence of intellectual insanity than every sinner does of moral insanity. If bedlam itself furnishes evidence that its inhabitants are intellectually crazy, then so does every sinner that he is morally mad.

Making Salvation More Difficult

Sinners act as if they were afraid to be saved. Often they seem to be trying to make their salvation as difficult as possible. For example, many of them know what Christ has said about the danger of riches and the difficulty of saving rich men. They have read from His lips, *"How hard it is for those who have riches to enter the kingdom of God!"* (Mark 10:23), and *"It is easier for a camel to go through the eye of a needle than for a rich man to enter the kingdom of God"* (v. 25). This they know, and yet how many of them are in a mad rush to be rich! For this end, some are ready to sacrifice their consciences—some their health—and all seem deliberately ready to sacrifice even their souls! How could they more certainly ensure their own damnation?

Thus they regard damnation as if it were salvation, and salvation as if it were damnation. They rush toward damnation as if it were heaven, and flee salvation as if it were hell.

Is this an exaggeration? No; this is only the simple truth. Sinners rush along the pathway to hell as if it were the chief good of their existence, and they shun the way to heaven as if it were the consummation of evil. Sinner, this is your own moral state. The picture that I have drawn here gives only the naked facts of the case, without exaggeration.

Pure Wickedness

This moral insanity is a state of pure wickedness. The special feature of it that makes it a guilty state is that it is altogether voluntary. It results not from the loss of reason, but from the abuse of reason. The will persists in acting against reason and conscience. Despite the affirmations of reason, and regardless of the admonitions of conscience, the sinner presses on in his career of rebellion against God and goodness. In such voluntary wickedness, guilt is intrinsically involved.

Besides, this action is often deliberate. The man sins in his cool, deliberate moments as well as in his excited moments. If he sins most overtly and boldly in his excited moments, he does not repent and change his position toward God in his deliberate moments; rather, he virtually endorses the hasty purposes of his more excited hours. This heightens his guilt.

Obstinate and Unyielding in Sin

The wicked man's purposes of sin are also obstinate and unyielding. In ten thousand ways, God is influencing his mind to change his purposes, but usually in vain. This career of sin is in violation of all man's obligations. Who does not know this? The sinner never acts from right motives, never yields to the sway of a sense of obligation, never practically recognizes his obligation to love his neighbor as himself or to honor the Lord his God.

His behavior reflects a total rejection of both God's law and the Gospel. The law he will not obey; the Gospel of pardon he will not accept. He seems determined to brave the omnipotence of Jehovah, and to dare His vengeance. Is he not mad with his idols? (See Jeremiah 50:38.) Is it saying too much when the Bible affirms, *"Madness is in their heart while they live"*?

REMARKS

1. Sinners strangely accuse believers of being mad and crazy. Just as soon as Christian people begin to act as if the truth they believe is a reality, then wicked men cry out, "See, they are getting crazy." Yet those very sinners often admit that the Bible is true. They also often admit that the things Christians believe to be true are really so. Further still, they often admit that those Christians are doing only what they ought to do, and are acting only as the sinners themselves ought to act. Still, they charge Christians with insanity. It is odd that even those sinners themselves know these Christians to be the only rational men on the earth. I saw this plainly before my conversion. I knew then that Christians were the only people in all the world who had any valid claim to be considered sane.

2. If intellectual insanity is a shocking fact, how much more so is moral insanity? I have already mentioned my first impressions upon seeing one who was intellectually insane, but a case of moral insanity ought to be deemed far more distressing and astounding. Suppose a respected religious leader were to become a madman. People throughout the country would become solemn and pensive. "What!" they would say. "That leader, that great man—a madman? How the mighty have fallen! What a horrible sight!"

But how much more horrible to see that man become a moral madman—to see a selfish heart running wild with his gigantic intellect, to see his moral principles fading away before the demands of selfish ambition, to see such a man become a drunkard, a carouser, a loafer. If this were to occur in a religious leader, how inexpressibly shocking! Intellectual madness cannot even be compared with this!

3. Although some sinners may be externally reasonable and may seem to be generally agreeable in temperament and character, every real sinner is actually insane. In view of all the solemnities of eternity, he insists on being controlled only by the things of time. With the powers of an angel, he aims only at the low pursuits of a selfish heart. Angels must look on such a case with pure sadness! Eternity so vast, and its issues so dreadful, yet this sinner drives furiously to hell as if he were on the highway to heaven! And all this only because he is infatuated with *"the pleasures of sin for a season"* (Heb. 11:25 KJV). At first, he seems to have really mistaken hell for heaven; but on a closer examination, you see it is no real mistake of the intellect. He knows very well the difference between hell and heaven, but he is deluding himself under the impulses of his mad heart! The mournful fact is that he loves sin, and so he pursues it eagerly. He is so insane that he rushes greedily toward his own damnation, just as if he were in pursuit of heaven!

We shudder at the thought that any of our friends are becoming idiotic or lunatic. But this is not half so bad as to have one of them become wicked. Better to have a whole family become idiotic than to have one of them become a hardened sinner. Indeed, the former, compared with the latter, is nothing, for the lunatic will not always be so. When the mortal body is laid away in the grave, the soul

135

may look out again in the free air of liberty, as if it had never been locked in a dark prison. The body, too, will be raised again, to bloom in eternal vigor and beauty. However, moral insanity only grows worse and worse forever! The root of this condition is not in a diseased brain, but in a diseased heart and soul; death cannot cure it. The resurrection will only raise the sinner to *"shame and everlasting contempt"* (Dan. 12:2), and the eternal world will only give wider scope to his madness, so that it will rage on with augmented vigor forever.

Some people are more afraid of being called insane than of being called wicked. Surely they show the fatal delusion that is in their hearts. Intellectual insanity is only pitiable, not disgraceful; but moral insanity is unspeakably disgraceful. No one should wonder that God says, *"Some* [will awake] *to shame and everlasting contempt"* (v. 2).

Conversion to God is becoming morally sane. It consists in restoring the will and the inclinations to the proper control of the intelligence, the reason, and the conscience. This puts the man once more in harmony with himself—all his faculties adjusted to their true positions and proper functions.

Sometimes people relapse into intellectual insanity after being apparently quite restored. This is a sad case, and it brings sorrow upon the hearts of friends. Yet in no case can it be so sad as a case of backsliding into moral insanity. People who have become converted, but not well established, sometimes backslide into moral insanity.

An insane asylum is a mournful place. How can a heart with any human sensitivity contemplate such a scene without intense grief? As you pass through the halls of an insane asylum, you see the traces of intellectual ruin; there is a noble-looking woman, perfectly insane; there is a man of splendid demeanor and conduct—all in ruins! How dreadful! But if this is so awful, what a place hell must be! These insane asylums are frightful; how much more the asylums of the morally insane!

Suppose you were to visit a lunatic asylum in Ohio, to go around to all its wards and study the case of each patient. Then you visit another asylum in Indiana, and another in New York, until you have visited asylums in all fifty states of the United States. Then you go to London and visit its asylum. Would not all these scenes be mournful? Would you not cry out long before you had finished, "Enough! Enough! How can I bear to look upon these madmen? How can I endure to behold such desolation?"

Suppose, then, you next go to the great moral insane asylum of the universe—the hell of lost souls—for if men will make themselves mad, God must shut them up in one vast asylum. Why should He not? The well-being of His empire demands that all the moral insanity of His kingdom be withdrawn from the society of the holy, and shut up separately. In this place will be those whose intellects are right, but whose hearts are all wrong. Ah, what a place must that be in which to spend one's eternity! The great mad-house of the universe!

Sometimes sinners, aware of their own insanity, get glimpses of this fearful state while they are yet on earth. When I got the idea that Christians are the only people who can claim to be rational, I asked myself, "Why should I not become a Christian? Would it hurt me to obey God? Would it ruin my peace or damage my prospects for either this life or the next? Why do I go on so?"

I said to myself, "I can give no account of it, only that I am mad. All I can say is that my heart is set on iniquity, and will not turn."

Poor maniac! Not unfortunate, but wicked! How many of you know that this is your real case? Oh, young man, did your father think you were sane when he sent you to church last Sunday? You were intellectually sane, perhaps, but not morally. As to your moral nature, all was utterly deranged. My dear young friend, does your own moral course commend itself to your conscience and your reason? If not, what are you but a moral maniac? Young man, young woman, must you not in truth write yourselves down as moral maniacs?

4. Finally, the subject shows the importance of not quenching the Spirit, who is God's agent for curing moral maniacs. Oh, if you put out His light from your souls, there remains to you only *"the blackness of darkness forever"* (Jude 13)! A young man at Lane Seminary, dying in his sins, said to me, "Why did you not tell me there is such a thing as eternal damnation? Well, why did you not tell me?" I had told him. "Oh, I am going there—how can I die so? It's growing dark; bring in a light!" And so he passed away from this world of light and hope.

O sinner, take care that you do not put out the light that God has cast into your dark heart, lest, when you pass away, your surroundings will grow dark to your soul at midday—the opening into *"the blackness of darkness forever."*

Seven

Conditions of Being Saved

What must I do to be saved?
—Acts 16:30

The circumstances that gave occasion to the words of the above Scripture verse were briefly the following. Paul and Silas had gone to Philippi to preach the Gospel. Their preaching excited great opposition and tumult; they were arrested and thrown into prison, and the jailer was charged to keep them safely. At midnight, as they were praying and singing praises, God came down. The earth quaked, the prison rocked, its doors burst open, and the prisoners' chains fell off. The jailer sprang up and, supposing his prisoners had fled, was about to take his own life—before he could be killed himself for allowing the prisoners to escape. But then Paul cried out, *"Do yourself no harm, for we are all here"* (Acts 16:28). The jailer then *"called for a light, ran in, and fell down trembling before Paul and Silas. And he brought them out and said, 'Sirs, what must I do to be saved?'"* (vv. 29–30).

Now, knowing the story behind our text verse, I will show, first, what sinners must not do to be saved, and second, what they must do.

139

What Sinners Must Not Do to Be Saved

It has now come to be necessary and very important to tell men what they must not do in order to be saved. When the Gospel was first preached, Satan had not introduced as many delusions to mislead people as he has now. At that time, it was enough to give the simple and direct answer, as Paul did, telling men only what they must do at once. But this does not seem to be enough now. So many delusions and perversions have bewildered and darkened the minds of men that they often need a great deal of instruction to lead them back to the simple views of the subject that prevailed at first. Therefore, it is important to show sinners what they must not do if they intend to be saved.

Imagine That You Have Nothing to Do

First, you must not imagine that you have nothing to do in this matter. In Paul's time, nobody seemed to have thought of this. At that time, the doctrine of Universalism was not much developed. People had not begun to dream that they could be saved without doing anything. They had not learned the idea that sinners have nothing to do to be saved. If this idea, so common today, had been popular in Philippi, the question of our text verse would not have been asked. No trembling sinner would have cried out, *"What must I do to be saved?"*

If sinners imagine they have nothing to do, they are never likely to be saved. Falsehood and lies cannot save men's souls, and surely nothing is more false than this idea. Sinners know that they have to do something to be saved. Why, then, do they pretend that everyone will be saved whether they do their duty or constantly refuse to do it? The very idea is preposterous and is entertained only by the most obvious outrage against both common sense and an enlightened conscience.

Mistake What Is to Be Done

Second, you should not mistake what you have to do. The duty required of sinners is very simple, and it would be easily understood, if it were not for the false ideas that prevail as to what religion is and as to the exact things that God requires as conditions of salvation. On these points, erroneous opinions prevail to a most alarming extent. Hence the danger of mistake. Beware lest you be deceived in a matter of such vital importance.

Assume That You Are Unable

Third, do not say or imagine that you cannot do what God requires. On the contrary, always assume that you can. If you assume that you cannot, this very assumption will be fatal to your salvation.

Put Off Your Decision

Fourth, do not procrastinate. If you ever intend or hope to be saved, you must set yourself against this most pernicious delusion. Probably no other mode of evading present duty has ever prevailed so extensively as this, or has destroyed so many souls. Almost all men in Christendom intend to prepare for death—intend to repent and become religious before they die. Even Universalists expect to become religious at some time—perhaps after death, or perhaps after being purified from their sins by purgatorial fires—but *somehow* they expect to become holy, for they know they must before they can see God and enjoy His presence. But you will see that they put off this matter of becoming holy to the most distant time possible. Feeling a strong dislike to it now, they flatter themselves that God will make sure that it is done in due time in the next world, no matter how much they may frustrate His efforts to do it in this world. As long as it remains in their power to choose whether to become holy or not, they use the time to enjoy their sin, and they leave it with God to make them holy in the next world.

So sinners by the thousands press their way down to hell under this delusion. Often, when faced with the claims of God, they will even name the time when they will repent. It may be very near—perhaps as soon as they get home from the meeting, or as soon as the sermon is over. Or it may be more remote, as, for example, when they have finished their education, or become settled in life, or have bought a little more property, or are ready to abandon some business of questionable morality. But whether the time is near or remote, the delusion is fatal—the thought of procrastination is murder to the soul.

Such sinners are little aware that Satan himself has poured out his spirit upon them and is leading them wherever he wants them to go. He cares little whether they put off salvation for a longer time or a shorter time. If he can persuade them to delay for a long time, he likes it well; if there is only a short delay, he feels quite sure he can renew the delay and get another extension—so it answers his purpose fully in the end.

Now, sinner, if you ever intend to be saved, you must resist this spirit of Satan. You must cease to procrastinate. You can never be converted as long as you continue to delay and to promise yourself that you will become religious at some future time. Did procrastination ever accomplish any important business in your earthly affairs?

The sinner accomplishes nothing but his own ruin so long as he procrastinates. Until he says, "Now is my time; today I will do all my duty," he is only playing the fool and laying up his wages accordingly. (See Romans 6:23.) Oh, it is infinite madness to defer a matter of such vast interest and of such perilous uncertainty!

Wait for God to Do Your Duty

Fifth, if you wish to be saved, you must not wait for God to do what He commands you to do. God will surely do all that He can for your salvation. All that the nature of the case allows Him to do, He either has done or stands ready to do as soon as your position and course will allow Him to do it. Long before you were born, He anticipated your needs as a sinner, and He began on the most liberal scale to make provision for them. He gave His Son to die for you, thus doing all that needed to be done by way of an atonement. For a long time, He has been shaping His providence in order to give you the necessary knowledge of duty. He has sent you His Word and Spirit. Indeed, He has given you the highest possible evidence that He will be energetic and prompt on His part—He will earnestly work for your salvation. *You know this.* What sinner among you fears that God will be negligent in the matter of his salvation?

Not one. No, many of you are rather annoyed that God presses you so earnestly and is so energetic in the work of securing your salvation. Can you quiet your conscience with the excuse of waiting for God to do your duty?

The fact is, there are things you must do that God cannot do for you. He cannot and will not do Himself the things that He has decreed and revealed as the conditions of your salvation. If He could have done them Himself, He would not have asked you to do them. Every sinner ought to consider this. God requires you to repent and have faith because it is naturally impossible for anyone else but you to do these things. They are your own personal matters—the voluntary exertions of your own mind—and no other being in heaven, earth, or hell can do these things for you in your place. As far as substitution was naturally possible, God has brought it into the equation, as in the case of the Atonement. He has never hesitated to meet and to bear all the self-denials that the work of salvation has involved.

Wait for God to Do Anything

Sixth, if you intend to be saved, you must not wait for God to do anything whatsoever. There is nothing to be waited for. God has either done all that He can already, or if anything more remains, He is ready and waiting this moment for you to do your duty so that He may impart all the necessary grace.

Don't wait for God to change your heart. Why should you wait for Him to do what He has commanded you to do? He waits for you to obey His command.

Flee to a Refuge of Lies

Seventh, do not flee to any *"refuge of lies"* (Isa. 28:17). Lies cannot save you. It is truth, not lies, that alone can save. God says you must be *"sanctified by the truth"* (John 17:19). I have often wondered how people could suppose that Universalism could save anyone. Sinners must be sanctified by the truth. There is no plainer teaching in the Bible than this, and no Bible doctrine is better sustained by reason.

Does Universalism sanctify anybody? Universalists say you must be punished for your sins, that this is the way in which sins will be put away—as if the fires of purgatory can thoroughly consume all sin and make the sinner pure. Is this being sanctified by the truth? You might as well hope to be saved by eating liquid fire! You might as well expect fire to purify your soul from sin in this world, as in the next! Why not?

It is amazing that men hope to be sanctified and saved by this great error—or, indeed, by any error. Suppose you could believe this delusion; would it make you holy? Do you believe it would make you humble, heavenly minded, sin-hating, benevolent? Can you believe any such thing? Be assured that Satan is only the father of lies (John 8:44) and not a savior. He cannot save you—in fact, he would not save you if he could. He intends his lies to destroy your soul, and nothing could be more adapted to his purpose than lies. Lies are only the natural poison of the soul. You take them at your peril!

Seek a Self-Indulgent Method of Salvation

Eighth, don't seek any self-indulgent method of salvation. The great effort among sinners has always

145

been to be saved by some way of self-indulgence. They are slow to admit that self-denial is indispensable to salvation—that total, unqualified self-denial is the condition of being saved. I warn you against supposing that you can be saved in some easy, self-pleasing way. Sinners ought to know that selfishness must be utterly put away and its demands resisted and put down.

The longer I live, the more fully I see that the Gospel system is the only one that can both meet the demands of the human intelligence and supply the needs of man's sinning, depraved heart. The duties that the sinner must fulfill are just the things that I know are naturally the conditions of salvation. Why, then, should any sinner think of being saved on any other conditions? Why desire it, even if it were possible?

Think That Another Time Will Be Better

Ninth, don't imagine you will ever have a more favorable time than the present. Impenitent sinners are prone to imagine that the present is not nearly as convenient a season as may be expected later. So they put off their decision, in hope of a better time. They think that they will have more conviction, fewer obstacles, or fewer hindrances later on. Felix, the governor of Judea in Paul's day, thought this way. He did not intend to do without salvation any more than you do, but he was very busy just then. He had certain matters that seemed pressing, so he begged to be excused on the promise of giving attention to the subject as soon as it became more convenient. But did the convenient season ever come? Never. Nor does it ever come to those who

similarly resist God's solemn call and grieve away
His Spirit.

Thousands are now waiting in the pains of hell
who said just as Felix did, *"Go away for now; when I
have a convenient time I will call for you"* (Acts
24:25). Oh, sinner, when will your convenient season
come? Are you aware that no season will ever be
"convenient" for you unless God calls your attention
earnestly and solemnly to the subject? And can you
expect Him to do this when *you* want Him to, especially when you scorn His call each time He chooses
to call you? Have you not heard Him say,

> *Because I have called and you refused, I have
> stretched out my hand and no one regarded,
> because you disdained all my counsel, and
> would have none of my rebuke, I also will
> laugh at your calamity; I will mock when your
> terror comes, when your terror comes like a
> storm, and your destruction comes like a
> whirlwind, when distress and anguish come
> upon you. Then they will call on me, but I will
> not answer; they will seek me diligently, but
> they will not find me.* (Prov. 1:24–28)

O sinner, this will be a fearful and a final doom! And
the myriad voices of God's universe will say,
"Amen."

Suppose That Another Time Will Be As Good

Tenth, do not suppose that you will find another
time as good, or one in which you can repent just as
well as now. Many people are ready to suppose that,
although there may be no better time for themselves,

there will at least be one that is as good. Vain delusion! Sinner, you already owe ten thousand talents! (See Matthew 18:24.) Will it be just as easy to be forgiven of this debt while you show that you don't care how much and how long you prolong it? In a case like this, where everything depends upon your securing the goodwill of your creditor, do you hope to gain it by positively insulting Him to His face?

Or look at the case from another perspective. You know that your heart must one day repent for sin, or you will be forever damned. You also know that each successive sin increases the hardness of your heart and makes it more difficult for you to repent. How, then, can you reasonably hope that a future time will be equally favorable for your repentance? When you have hardened your heart like a stone, can you hope that repentance will still be as easy to you as ever?

Sinner, you know that God requires you to break off from your sins *now*. But you look into His face and say to Him, "Lord, it is just as well for me to stop abusing You at some future time, when it is more convenient for me. As long as I will be saved in the end, I will think it all my gain to go on insulting and abusing You as long as I can. And since You are so very compassionate and long-suffering, I think I may venture on in sin and rebellion against You for many more months and years. Lord, don't hurry me; let me have my way; let me humiliate You and spit in Your face. It will all end up the same as long as I repent in time to be finally saved. Indeed, I know that You are earnestly asking me to repent now, but I much prefer to wait a season, and it will be just as well for me to repent at some future time."

And now, do you suppose that God will set His seal to this—that He will say, "You are right, sinner, I set my seal of approval upon your course. It is well that you have this perspective on your duty to your Maker and your Father. Go on; your course will ensure your salvation"? Do you expect this type of response from God?

Wait for Others to Approve

Eleventh, if you ever expect to be saved, don't wait to see what others will do or say. I was recently astonished to find that a young lady who was under conviction was quite troubled about what her brother would think of her if she were to give her heart to God. She knew her duty, but her brother was impenitent. She would come before God and say, "O great God, I know I ought to repent, but I can't, for I don't know whether my brother will like it. I know that he, too, is a sinner, and must repent or lose his soul, but I am much more afraid of his disapproval than I am of Yours. I care more for his praise than I do for Yours; consequently, I dare not repent until he does!" How shocking this is! I find it strange that, regarding this important subject, people will always ask, "What will others say of me?" Are you obedient to God? What, then, can others have to say about your duty to Him? God requires repentance not only from you but also from them. Why don't you do it at once?

Not long ago, when I was preaching overseas, one of the influential men of the city came to the inquiry meeting, apparently much convicted and in great distress for his soul. But being a man of high political standing, and supposing himself to be very dependent upon his friends, he insisted that he must consult them and have a regard for their feelings in this matter. I could not get him to think any differently, although I spent three hours trying to do so. He seemed almost ready to repent—I thought he certainly would—but he slipped away, and I expect he will be found at last among the lost in perdition. Is not such a result to be expected, when he tore himself away from his duty because of an excuse like that?

O sinner, you must not care what others say of you—let them say what they please. Remember, the question is between your own soul and God, and *"if you are wise, you are wise for yourself, and if you scoff, you will bear it alone"* (Prov. 9:12). You must die for yourself, and for yourself you must appear before God in judgment! Go, young woman, ask your brother, "Can you answer for me when I come to the Judgment? Can you pledge yourself that you can stand in my place and answer for me there?" Until you have reason to believe that he can, it is wise for you to disregard his opinions if they stand in your way at all. Whoever puts forth any objection to your immediate repentance, do not fail to ask him, "Can you shield my soul in the Judgment? If I can be assured that you can and will, I will make you my savior; but if not, then I must attend to my own salvation and leave you to attend to yours."

I will never forget the scene that occurred while my own mind was contemplating this great point. Seeking a quiet place for prayer, I went into a wooded area, found a perfectly secluded spot behind some large logs, and knelt down. Suddenly, a leaf rustled, and I sprang up, thinking that somebody must be coming and I would be seen praying. I had not been aware that I cared what others said of me, but as, at the time, I looked back upon my thoughts, I could see that I did care infinitely too much what others thought of me.

Closing my eyes again for prayer, I heard a rustling leaf again, and then the thought came over me like a wave of the sea, "I am ashamed of confessing my sin, ashamed of being found speaking with God!" Oh, how ashamed I felt of this embarrassment! I can never describe the strong and overpowering impression that this thought made on my mind. I cried aloud at the very top of my voice, for I felt that, though all the men on earth and all the devils in hell might be present to hear and see me, I would not shrink and would not cease to cry to God. What is it to me if others see me seeking the face of my God and Savior? I am hurrying to the Judgment, and there I will not be ashamed to have the Judge as my friend. There, I will not be ashamed to have sought His face and His pardon on earth. There, no one can shrink away from the gaze of the universe. Oh, how gladly sinners would shrink away at the Judgment if they could, but they cannot! Nor can they stand there in each other's places to answer for each other's sins.

Young woman, can you say at the Judgment, "Oh, my brother, you must answer for me, for I rejected Christ and lost my soul in order to please you"? That brother is himself a guilty rebel—confused, agonized, and faltering before the awful Judge. How can he befriend you in such an awful hour? Do not fear his displeasure now, but rather warn him, while you can, to escape for his life before

151

the wrath of the Lord grows hot against him and there is no remedy.

Indulge Prejudices against Religion

Twelfth, if you desire to be saved, you must not indulge prejudices against God, against His ministers, against Christians, or against anything that is of God. Some people are greatly in danger of losing their souls because they are inclined toward strong prejudices. Once they have committed against any persons or things, they are highly likely to never again be truly honest with themselves about the matter of their salvation. Especially if these persons or things are connected with Christianity, the effect can be nothing else than ruinous. Their prejudices prevent them from ever fulfilling the great conditions of salvation, for it is indispensable to salvation that they be entirely honest. Their souls must act before God in the open sincerity of truth, or they cannot be converted.

I have known people in revivals to remain a long time under great conviction, without submitting themselves to God. By carefully questioning them, I have found them to be entirely hedged in by their prejudices, and yet they were so blind to this fact that they would not admit that they had any prejudice at all. In my observation of convicted sinners, I have found this to be one of the most common obstacles in the way of the salvation of souls. Men become committed against Christianity, and while they remain in this state, it is naturally impossible for them to repent. Yet God will not humor their prejudices or lower His conditions of salvation to accommodate their feelings.

Remain Unforgiving

You must give up all hostile feelings in cases where you have been injured. Sometimes I have seen people shut out from the kingdom of heaven because they would not forgive and forget. Instead, they maintained such a spirit of resistance and revenge that they could not repent of the sin toward God, nor could God forgive them. Of course, they lost heaven. I have heard men say, "I cannot forgive; I will not forgive. I have been injured, and I never will forgive that wrong." You must not hold on to such feelings; if you do, you cannot be saved.

Let Others' Prejudices Dictate Your Actions

Again, you must not allow yourself to stumble because of the prejudices of others. I have often been astounded by the state of things in families, where the parents had prejudices against the minister and began to lay stumbling blocks before their children, eventually to the ruin of their children's souls. This is often the true reason that children are not converted. Their minds are turned against the Gospel by being turned against those from whom they hear it preached. I would rather have people come into my family and curse and swear before my children than to have them speak against those who preach the Gospel to them. Therefore, I say to all parents, take care what you say, if you do not wish to shut the gate of heaven against your children!

Take a Position That Keeps You from Your Duty

You also must not allow yourself to take some fixed position, and then permit the stand you have taken to bar you from performing any obvious duty before God. People sometimes allow themselves to be committed against taking what is called "the anxious seat." They will not publicly admit that they are concerned for the salvation of their souls. Consequently, they refuse to go forward under circumstances when it is obviously proper that they should, and their refusal places them in an attitude unfavorable, and perhaps fatal, to their conversion. Let every sinner beware of this!

Hold On to Questionable Practices

Dear reader, do not hold on to anything about which you have any doubt of its lawfulness or propriety. Cases often occur in which people are not fully satisfied that a thing is wrong, and yet are not satisfied that it is right. In cases of this sort, it should not be enough to say, "Some Christians do this thing." You ought to have better reasons than this for your course of conduct. If you ever expect to be saved, you must abandon all practices that you even suspect to be wrong. This principle seems to be involved in the passage, *"He who doubts is condemned if he eats, because he does not eat from faith; for whatever is not from faith is sin"* (Rom. 14:23). To do what is of doubtful propriety is to allow yourself to tamper with the divine authority, and this will certainly break down in your mind the solemn fear of sinning—a fear that you must carefully cherish if you will ever be saved.

Wait for Christians to Be Better than They Are

If you wish to be saved, do not look at professing Christians and wait for them to become as involved as they should be in the great work of God. If they are not what they ought to be, let them alone. Let them bear their own responsibility. Convicted sinners often compare themselves with professing Christians, and they excuse themselves for delaying their duty, because these Christians are delaying theirs. Sinners must not do this if they wish to be saved. It is very probable that you will always find enough guilty believers to stumble over into hell, if you will allow yourself to do so.

On the other hand, many professing Christians may not be nearly so bad as you suppose, and you must not be so critical, giving the worst interpretation of their conduct. You have other work to do than this. Let them stand or fall on their own. Unless you abandon the practice of picking out flaws in the conduct of professing Christians, it is utterly impossible that you will be saved.

Depend on the Prayers of Christians

Again, do not depend on the prayers or influence of believers in any way. I have known children to depend a long time on the prayers of their parents, putting those prayers in the place of Jesus Christ, or at least in the place of their own present efforts to do their duty. This course pleases Satan entirely. Therefore, depend on no prayers—not even those of the holiest Christians on earth. The matter of your conversion lies between yourself and God alone, as if you were the only sinner in all the world, or as if there were no other beings in the universe but yourself and your God. (See Philippians 2:12.)

Seek Any Defense, Excuse, or Stumbling Block

Do not seek any defense or excuse whatsoever. I dwell upon this and urge it all the more because I so often find people unknowingly resting on some excuse. In conversing with them about their spiritual state, I see this and say, "You are resting on that excuse." "Am I?" they say. "I did not know it."

Do not seek stumbling blocks for the purpose of self-vindication. Sinners often do this. All at once they become wide awake to the faults of professing believers. The real fact is, they are all looking for something to which they can take exception, so that they can blunt the keen edge of truth upon their own consciences. This never helps along their own salvation.

Tempt God's Patience

Do not tempt the patience of God. If you do, you are in the utmost danger of being given over to Satan forever. Do not presume that you may go on even longer in your sins, and still find the gate of mercy. This presumption has paved the way for the ruin of many souls.

Lose Hope of Being Saved

Do not lose all hope of salvation and settle down in unbelief, saying, "There is no mercy for me." You must not despair to the point of shutting yourself out from the kingdom of God. You may well lose hope of ever being saved apart from Christ and apart from repentance, but you are required to believe the Gospel. To do this is to believe the glad tidings that Jesus Christ has come to save sinners, even the chief of sinners, and that *the one who comes to* [Him, He] *will by no means cast out*" (John 6:37). You have no right to disbelieve this and to act as if there were no truth in it.

Wait for More Conviction

You must not wait for more conviction. Why do you need any more? You know your guilt and your present duty. Nothing can be more preposterous, therefore, than to wait for more conviction. If you did not know that you are a sinner, or that you are guilty for sin, there might be some sense in seeking more conviction of the truth on these points.

Wait for Different Feelings

Do not wait for more or different feelings. Sinners are often saying, "I must feel differently before I can come to Christ," or "I must have more feeling"—as if this were the great thing that God requires of them. In this they are altogether mistaken.

Think You Must Be Better Prepared

Do not wait to be better prepared. While you wait, you are growing worse and worse and are quickly making your salvation impossible.

Try to Make Yourself Look Better

Don't try, by prayers or tears or by anything else whatsoever, to make yourself appear better before God. Do you suppose that your prayers put God under any obligation to forgive you? Suppose you owed a man $500, and you went a hundred times a week to beg him to forgive you of this debt. Then suppose you began to pray to God against your creditor, as if you had a claim against him. Suppose you tried to pursue this course until you had canceled the debt. Could you hope to prove anything by this course except that you were insane? And yet sinners seem to think that their many prayers and tears put the Lord under real obligation to them to forgive them.

Rely on Anything except Christ

Never rely on anything else besides Jesus Christ and Him crucified. (See 1 Corinthians 2:2.) It is preposterous for you to hope, as many do, to make some atonement by your own sufferings. In my early experience, I thought I could not expect to be converted at once, but must suffer a long time. I said to myself, "God will not pity me until I feel worse than I do now. I can't expect Him to forgive me until I feel a greater agony in my soul than this." Even if I could have gone on prolonging my sufferings until they equaled the miseries of hell, they could not have changed God. The fact is, God does not ask you to suffer. Your sufferings cannot serve as atonement. Why, therefore, should you attempt to throw aside the system that God has provided and to bring in one of your own?

Be Willing to Suffer rather than Submit

There is another view of the case. The thing God demands of you is that you should bow your stubborn will to Him. Think of a disobedient child, required to submit, who resorts to weeping and groaning and even torturing himself in the hope of moving the pity of his father. Meanwhile, he still refuses to submit to parental authority. He would be very glad to suffer rather than submit. This is what the sinner is doing but must not do. He would gladly put his own sufferings in the place of submission to God, and he would rather move the pity of the Lord so much that God would withdraw the hard condition of repentance and submission.

Pay Attention to Those Who Pity You

If you wish to be saved, you must not listen at all to those who pity you—those who supposedly take your part against God and try to make you think you are not as bad as you are. I once knew a woman who, after a long season of distressing conviction, fell into great despair. Her health deteriorated, and she seemed about to die. All this time she found no relief but seemed only to become worse and worse, sinking down in awful despair. Her friends, instead of dealing plainly and faithfully with her and probing her guilty heart to the bottom, had taken the course of pitying her. They almost complained that the Lord would not have compassion on the poor, agonized woman.

At length, as this woman seemed to be in the last stages of life—so weak that she was scarcely able to speak in a low voice—there arrived a minister who better understood how to deal with convicted sinners. The woman's friends cautioned him to deal very carefully with her, as she was in a dreadful state and was greatly to be pitied. But he saw that it would be best to deal with her very faithfully. As he approached her bedside, she raised her faint voice and begged for a little water. He said to her, "Unless you repent, you will soon be where there is not a drop of water to cool your tongue." "Oh," she cried, "must I go down to hell?" "Yes, you must, and you soon will, unless you repent and submit to God. Why don't you repent and submit immediately?" "Oh," she replied, "it is an awful thing to go to hell!" "Yes, and for that very reason God has provided an atonement through Jesus Christ, but you won't accept it. He brings the cup of salvation to your lips, and you push it away. Why do you do this? Why do you persist in being an enemy of God and scorn His offered salvation, when you might become His friend and have salvation?"

This was the gist of their conversation, and its result was that the woman saw her guilt and her duty. Turning to the Lord, she found pardon and peace.

Therefore, if your conscience convicts you of sin, don't let anybody take your part against God. Your wound does not need a bandage, but a probe. Don't fear the probe; it is the only thing that can save you. Don't try to hide your guilt, to veil your eyes from seeing it. Don't be afraid to know the worst, for you must know the very worst, and the sooner you know it the better. I warn you, don't try to find some physician who will give you a drug, for you don't need it. Just as you would avoid death itself, shun all those who speak to you smooth things and prophesy deceits. (See Isaiah 30:10.) They will surely ruin your soul.

Think That Christianity Will Interfere with Life

Again, do not suppose that if you become a Christian, it will interfere with any of the necessary or appropriate duties of life or with anything to which you ought to attend. Religion never interferes with any real duty. In fact, a proper attention to your various duties is indispensable to your being religious.

Pay Attention to Anything That Will Hinder You

Furthermore, if you wish to be saved, you must not give heed to anything that will hinder you. It is infinitely important that your soul should be saved. No consideration thrown in your way should be allowed to have the weight of even a straw or a feather. Jesus Christ has illustrated this by several parables, especially in the one that compares the kingdom of heaven to *"a merchant seeking beautiful pearls, who, when he had found one pearl of great price, went and sold all that he had and bought it"* (Matt. 13:45–46). In another parable, the kingdom of heaven is said to be *"like treasure hidden in a field, which a man found and hid; and for joy over it he goes and sells all that he has and buys that field"* (v. 44). Through such examples, sinners are definitely taught that they must be ready to make any sacrifice that may be required in order to gain the kingdom of heaven.

Seek Religion for Your Own Gain

Again, you must not seek religion selfishly. You must not make your own salvation or happiness the supreme end. Beware, for if you make this your supreme end, you will get a false hope and will probably glide along down the pathway of the hypocrite into the deepest hell.

What Sinners Must Do to Be Saved

Now that I have expounded upon what sinners must not do in order to be saved, I will explain what sinners must do.

Understand What You Must Do

First, you must understand what you have to do. It is of the utmost importance that you see this clearly. You need to know that you must return to God, and you need to understand what this means. The difficulty between yourself and God is that you have stolen yourself and run away from His service. By right, you belong to God. He created you for Himself, and so He had a perfectly righteous claim to the homage of your heart and the service of your life. But you, instead of living to meet His claims, have run away, have withdrawn from God's service, and have lived to please yourself. Now your duty is to return and restore yourself to God.

Confess Your Sins to God and Man

Second, you must return and confess your sins to God. You must confess that you have been all wrong, and that God has been all right. Go before the Lord and lay open the depth of your guilt. Tell Him that you deserve just as much damnation as He has threatened.

These confessions are indispensable to your being forgiven. In accordance with this, the Lord says, *"If their uncircumcised hearts are humbled, and they accept their guilt; then I will remember My covenant"* (Lev. 26:41–42). Then God can forgive. But as long as you challenge this point and will not acknowledge that God is right, or will not admit that you are wrong, He can never forgive you.

Moreover, you must confess to man if you have injured anyone. Is it not a fact that you have injured someone—perhaps many of your fellowmen? Have you not slandered your neighbor and said things that you have no right to say? Have you not in some instances, which you could call to mind if you were willing, lied to them, or about them, or covered up or perverted the truth? Have you not been willing to give others false impressions of you or of your conduct? If so, you must renounce all such iniquity, for *"he who covers his sins will not prosper, but whoever confesses and forsakes them will have mercy"* (Prov. 28:13). Furthermore, you must not only confess your sins to God and to the people you have injured, but you must also make restitution. You have not taken the position of repentance before God and man until you have done this also. God cannot treat you as a penitent until you have done it.

I do not mean by this that God cannot forgive you until you have carried into effect your purpose of restitution by finishing the outward act, for sometimes it may demand time, and may in some cases be impossible to you. But the purpose must be sincere and thorough before you can be forgiven by God.

Renounce Yourself

Third, you must renounce yourself. This implies, first of all, that you must renounce your own righteousness, forever discarding the very idea of having any righteousness in yourself. It also implies that you must forever relinquish the idea of having done any good that can commend you to God or ever be considered as a basis for your justification. A third thing that is implied by this is that you must renounce your own will; you must always be ready to say not in word only, but also in heart, *"Your will be done on earth as it is in heaven"* (Matt. 6:10). You must consent most heartily that God's will will be your supreme law. Finally, this implies that you must renounce your way and let God have His way in everything. Never allow yourself to fret and be irritated by anything whatsoever. (See Matthew 6:25 and 1 Peter 5:7.) God's power extends to all events, and you ought to recognize His hand in all things; therefore, to worry about anything at all is to go against God, who has at least *permitted* that thing to occur as it has. Therefore, as long as you allow yourself to worry, you are not right with God.

You must become as a little child before God—subdued and trustful at His feet (Mark 10:15). The weather may be fair or foul, but you must let God have His way. Let all things go as they will, yet let God do as He pleases, and let it be your part to submit in perfect resignation. Until you take this position, you cannot be saved.

Fully Accept Christ as Your Savior

Fourth, you must come to Christ. You must accept Christ really and fully as your Savior. Renouncing all thought of depending on anything you have done or can do, you must accept Christ as your atoning Sacrifice, and as your ever living Mediator before God. Without the least limitation or reservation, you must place yourself under His wing as your Savior.

Seek to Please Christ above All Else

Fifth, you must seek supremely to please Christ and not yourself. It is impossible for you to be saved until you come into this attitude of mind—until you are so well pleased with Christ in all respects that you find your pleasure in doing Christ's pleasure. It is impossible for you to be happy in any other state of mind, or unhappy in this, for Christ's pleasure is infinitely good and right. Therefore, when His good pleasure becomes your good pleasure, and when your will harmonizes entirely with His, then you will be happy for the same reason that He is happy, and you cannot fail to be happy any more than Jesus Christ can. This becoming supremely happy in God's will is essentially the idea of salvation. In this state of mind, you are saved. Outside of it, you cannot be.

I have often been amazed that many professing Christians are deplorably and utterly mistaken on this point. Their real feeling is that Christ's service is an iron collar—an insufferably hard yoke. Hence, they work so hard to throw off some of this burden. They try to say that Christ does not require much, if any, self-denial; they say that Christ does not require much, if any, deviation from the course of worldliness and sin. Oh, if they could only get the standard of Christian duty quite down to a level with the fashions and customs of this world! How much easier it would then be to live a Christian life and to wear Christ's yoke! (See Matthew 11:29–30.)

But Christ's yoke as it really is, in their view, becomes an iron collar. Doing the will of Christ, instead of their own, is a hard business for them. Because doing His will is religion, they groan under the idea that they must be religious. Of these people I ask, "How much religion of this kind would it take to make hell?" Surely not much! When it gives you no joy to do God's pleasure, and yet you are required to do His pleasure in order to be saved, then you are perpetually forced into doing what you hate as the only means of escaping hell. Would not this be itself a hell? Can you not see that in this state of mind you are not saved and cannot be?

To be saved, you must come into a state of mind in which you ask no higher joy than to do God's pleasure. This alone will be forever enough to fill your cup to overflowing.

Have Complete Confidence in Christ

Sixth, you must have complete confidence in Christ, or you cannot be saved. You must absolutely believe in Him—believe all His words of promise. They were given to you to be believed, and unless you believe them, they can do you no good at all. Unless you exercise faith in them, they will not help you but will only aggravate your guilt for unbelief. God wants to be believed when He speaks in love to lost sinners. He gave them these *"exceedingly great and precious promises,"* so that by faith in them, they might escape *"the corruption that is in the world through lust"* (2 Pet. 1:4). But thousands of professing believers do not know how to use these promises; the promises might as well have been written on the sands of the sea.

Unbelievers will go down to hell in unbroken masses, unless they believe and take hold of God by faith in His promises. His awful wrath is surely against them! He says, *"'I would go through them, I would burn them together. Or let him take hold of My strength, that he may make peace with Me; and he shall make peace with Me'* (Isa. 27:4–5). Yes, let him stir up himself and take hold of My arm, strong to save, and then he may make peace with Me."* Do you ask how you may take hold? By faith. Yes, by faith; believe His words and take hold. Take hold of His strong arm, and don't be afraid any more than if there were no hell.

But you say, "I do believe, and yet I am not saved." No, you don't believe. A woman said to me, "I believe, I know I do, and yet here I am in my sins." "No," I said, "you don't. Do you have as much confidence in God as you would have in me if I had promised you a dollar? Do you ever pray to God? And if so, do you come with the same confidence as you would have if you came to me to ask for a dollar I had promised to give you? Until you have as much faith in God as this—until you have more confidence in God than you would have in ten thousand men—your faith does not honor God, and you cannot hope to please Him. You must say, *'Let God be true but every man a liar'* (Rom. 3:4)."

But you say, "Oh, I am a sinner. How can I believe?" I know you are a sinner, and so is everyone to whom God has given these promises. "Oh, but I am a *great* sinner!" you say. Well, Paul said, *"This is a faithful saying and worthy of all acceptance, that Christ Jesus came into the world to save sinners, of whom I am chief"* (1 Tim. 1:15). So you need not despair.

Forsake Everything That You Have

Seventh, you must forsake all that you have, or you cannot be Christ's disciple (Luke 14:33). There must be absolute and total self-denial.

By this I do not mean that you are never to eat again, or never again to clothe yourself, or never enjoy the society of your friends—no, not this. Rather, I mean that you should cease entirely from using any of these enjoyments selfishly. You must no longer think that you own yourself—your time, your possessions, or anything you have ever called your own. All these things you must now think of as God's, not yours. In this sense, you are to forsake all that you have, in the sense of laying everything on God's altar to be devoted supremely and only to His service.

When you come to God for pardon and salvation, come and lay everything you have at his feet. Come with your body, to offer it as a living sacrifice upon His altar. (See Romans 12:1.) Come with your soul and all its powers, and yield them in willing consecration to your God and Savior. Come, bring everything—body, soul, intellect, imagination, skills—everything, without holding back. You say, "Must I bring everything?" Yes, absolutely everything; do not keep back anything—don't sin against your own soul, like Ananias and Sapphira, by keeping back a part. (See Acts 5:1–10.) Rather, renounce your own claim to everything, and recognize God's right to all. Say, "Lord, these things are not mine. I had stolen them, but they were never mine. They were always Yours; I'll have them no longer. Lord, these things are all Yours, henceforth and forever. Now, what do You want me to do? I have no business of my own to do; I am wholly at Your disposal. Lord, what work do You have for me to do?"

In this spirit you must renounce the world, the flesh, and Satan. Your fellowship is henceforth to be with Christ, and not with those objects. You are to live for Christ, and not for the world, the flesh, or the Devil.

Believe What God Has Said about Christ

Eighth, you must believe the record God has given of His Son. He who does not believe does not receive the record, does not affirm that God is true. *"And this is the testimony* [record]: *that God has given us eternal life, and this life is in His Son"* (1 John 5:11). In order for you to have this life, you must believe the testimony, and of course you must act accordingly.

Suppose a poor man is living next door to you, and he receives a letter stating that a rich man has died in England, leaving him £100,000. A local bank informs him that he has received the amount on deposit, and the bank is waiting for his instructions. Well, the poor man says, "I can't believe this letter. I can't believe there ever was any such rich man; I can't believe there is £100,000 for me." So he lives and dies a poor man, because he won't believe the testimony.

This is just the case with the unbelieving sinner. God has given you eternal life, and it awaits your order; but you don't get it because you will not believe. You will not make out the order for it.

But you say, "I must have some feeling before I can believe. How can I believe until I have the feeling?" The poor man might say, "How can I believe that the £100,000 is mine? I do not have a penny of it now; I am as poor as ever." Yes, you are poor because you will not believe. If you would believe, you might go and buy out every store in this country. Still you cry, "I am as poor as ever. I can't believe it. Look at my poor worn clothes. I was never more ragged in my life; I do not have a particle of the feeling and the comforts of a rich man." Likewise, the sinner thinks he can't believe until he gets the inward experience! He must wait to have some of the feeling of a saved sinner before he can believe the record and take hold of the salvation! How preposterous! The poor man must wait to get his new clothes and fine house before he can believe a letter and draw upon his money! Of course he dooms himself to everlasting poverty, although mountains of gold were all his.

Sinner, you must understand this. Why should you be lost when eternal life has been bought and offered to you by the last will and testament of the Lord Jesus Christ? Will you not believe the record and draw upon the amount at once? For mercy's sake, understand this, and do not lose heaven by your own foolishness!

Accept Salvation from Sin

I must conclude by saying that, if you want to be saved, you must accept a prepared salvation, one already prepared and full and present. You must be willing to give up all your sins and be saved from them—now and forever. Until you agree to this, you cannot be saved at all. Many people would be willing to be saved in heaven, if they could hold on to some sins while on earth—or rather they *think* they would like heaven on such terms. But the fact is, they would dislike a pure heart and a holy life in heaven as much as they do on earth, and they utterly deceive themselves in supposing that they are ready or even willing to go to the heaven that God has prepared for His people. No, there can be no heaven except for those who accept a salvation from all sin in this world. They must take the Gospel as a system that holds no compromise with sin—a system that intends full deliverance from sin even now, and makes provision accordingly. Any other gospel is not the true one, and to accept Christ's Gospel in any other sense is not to accept it all. Its first and its last condition is *sworn and eternal renunciation of all sin.*

REMARKS

1. Recall that our text verse asks the question, *"What must I do to be saved?"* Paul did not give the same answer to this question that a Universalist would give. A Universalist would say, "You are to be saved by being first punished according to your sin. All men must expect to be punished." But this is not what Paul said. He would have been no comfort if he had answered in this manner: "You must all be punished according to the letter of the law you have broken." This could scarcely have been called *gospel,* for the very meaning of the word *gospel* is "good news."

Paul also did not say, as a Universalist would, "Do not concern yourself about this matter of being saved. It is sure enough that all men will be saved without any particular anxiety about it." No; Paul understood and did not hesitate to express the necessity of believing on the Lord Jesus Christ in order to be saved.

2. Take care that you do not sin willfully after saying that you have understood the truth concerning the way of salvation. Your danger of this increases as you see your duty more and more clearly. The most terrible damnation must fall on the heads of those who know their duty but who do not do it.

Therefore, when you are told plainly and truly what your duty is, be on your guard, lest you let salvation slip out of your hands. It may never come so near your reach again.

3. Do not wait, even an hour, before you obey God. Make up your mind now, at once, to accept the offer of salvation. Why not? Is it not the most reasonable course of action?

4. Let your mind focus on this great proposal and embrace it just as you would any other important proposition. God lays the proposition before you; you hear it explained, and you understand it. The next and only remaining step is to embrace it with all your heart. This is just like any other great question of life or death that might come before a community: the case is fully stated, the conditions are explained, and then the proposition is made. Will you accept it? Will you agree to meet the conditions? Do you heartily embrace the proposition? All this only makes sense.

The case of the sinner is similar. You understand the proposition. You know the conditions of salvation. You understand the contract into which you are to enter with your God and Savior. You agree to give your all to God—to lay yourself upon His altar to be used just as He pleases to use you. The only remaining question is, Will you agree to this at once? Will you go for full and everlasting consecration with all your heart?

5. The jailer in Acts 16 made no excuse. When he knew his duty, he yielded in a moment. Paul told him what to do, and he did it. He might have heard something about Paul's preaching before this night, but probably not much. But now he feared for his

life. How often I have been amazed by this case! This dark-minded heathen had probably heard a great deal of slander against these apostles, yet he came to them for the truth. As soon as he heard the truth, he was convinced; and being convinced, he yielded at once. Paul uttered a single sentence—*"Believe on the Lord Jesus Christ, and you will be saved, you and your household"* (Acts 16:31)—and the jailer received it, embraced it, and it was done.

Now, sinner, you know and acknowledge all this truth, and yet you will not at once believe and embrace it with all your heart. This is infinitely strange! Will not Sodom and Gomorrah rise up against you in the Judgment and condemn you? How could you bear to see that heathen jailer on that Day, and stand rebuked by his example there?

6. It is remarkable that Paul said nothing about the jailer's needing any help in order to believe and repent. He did not even mention the work of the Spirit, or allude to the jailer's need of it. Rather, Paul gave the jailer just the instruction that would most effectively secure the Spirit's aid and promote His action.

7. The jailer seems to have made no delay at all, waiting for no future or better time. As soon as the conditions were set before him, he yielded and embraced them. No sooner was the proposition made than he seized it.

I was once preaching in a village in New York, and there sat before me a lawyer who had been greatly offended by the Gospel. But that day I noticed that he sat leaning forward, as if he wanted to take hold of each word as it came forth. I was explaining and simplifying the Gospel, and I stated just how the

Gospel is offered to mankind. He said to me afterwards concerning what I had said, "I snatched at it; I put out my hand and seized it, and it became mine."

It was similar in my own case. While I was in the woods praying, after I had burst away from the fear of man, this passage came to mind: *"You will seek Me and find Me, when you search for Me with all your heart"* (Jer. 29:13). For the first time, I found that I believed a passage in the Bible. I had thought that I believed before, but surely I had never before believed as I now did. At this point I said to myself, "This is the Word of the everlasting God. My God, I take You at Your Word. You say that I will find You when I search for You with all my heart. Lord, I know that I search for You with all my heart." And true enough, I did find the Lord. Never in all my life was I more certain of anything than I was then that I had found the Lord.

This is the very idea of His promises—they were made to be believed, to be taken hold of as God's own words, and to be acted upon as if they actually mean just what they say. When God says, *"Look to Me, and be saved"* (Isa. 45:22), He wants us to look to Him as if He really had salvation in His hands to give, as well as a heart to give it. The true spirit of faith was well expressed by the psalmist: *"When You said, 'Seek My face,' my heart said to You, 'Your face, LORD, I will seek'"* (Ps. 27:8). This is the way—let your heart at once respond to the blessed words of invitation and of promise.

But you say, "I am not a Christian." And you never will be until you believe on the Lord Jesus Christ as your Savior. If you never become a Christian, the reason will be that you do not and will not

174

believe the Gospel and embrace it with all your heart.

The promises were made to be believed, and they belong to anyone who will believe them. They reach forth their precious words to all, and whoever desires to do so may take them as his own. Now, will you believe that the Father has given you eternal life? This is the fact declared; will you believe it?

You have now been told what you must not do and what you must do to be saved. Are you prepared to act? Do you say, "I am ready to renounce my own pleasure, and from now on seek no other pleasure than to please God"? Can you put aside everything else for the sake of this?

Sinner, do you want to please God, or will you choose to please yourself? Are you willing now to please God and to begin by believing on the Lord Jesus Christ for salvation? Will you be as simple-hearted as the Philippian jailer was? Will you act as promptly?

I demand your decision now. I dare not have you wait even an hour, lest you begin thinking or talking about something else and let slip these words of life and this precious opportunity to grasp an offered salvation. I am addressing every impenitent sinner. I call upon heaven and earth to record that I have set the Gospel before you here. Will you take it? Is it not reasonable for you to decide at once? Are you ready, now, to say before high heaven and before others, "I will renounce myself and yield to God! I am the Lord's, and let all men and angels bear witness that I am forevermore the Lord's"? Sinner, the infinite God waits for your consent!

Eight

The Sinner's Natural Power and Moral Weakness

*By whom a person is overcome, by him also
he is brought into bondage.*
—2 Peter 2:19

I n this chapter, I will discuss the moral state of the sinner. The first important fact to be noted is that all men are naturally free, and they are no less free for being sinners. They naturally have freedom of the will.

Human Beings Are Naturally Free

By the term *natural freedom,* I do not mean that they have a right to do as they please, for this can by no means be true. Nor do I mean that they are free agents merely in the sense of being *able* to do as they want to do. In fact, men sometimes can and sometimes cannot execute what they wish to do. But moral liberty does not consist in having the power to accomplish one's purposes.

Freedom of the will has often been defined as the power to do what you want to do, but for many reasons this meaning cannot be the true interpretation of freedom of the will. Consider the fact that *doing* depends upon physical, muscular action. Some of our muscles are not under the control of the will at all, while others are under its control. In regard to the muscles that can be controlled, all the freedom pertains to the will, not to the action of the muscles. The obedience of the muscles is absolute—it is not free or voluntary in any sense whatever. Hence, it is absurd to locate human freedom there.

This freedom is in the will itself, in its power of choice. To do or not to do—these are its options. By its own nature, the will has the function of determining its own choices. The soul wills to do or not to do; thus the soul is a moral ruler over its own activities. In this fact lies the foundation for *moral agency*. Any creature that can choose to do or not to do, and has knowledge and appreciation of its moral obligations, is a moral agent. No other creature can be.

I must especially call your attention to the fact that every man knows that he has a conscience, which tells him how he ought to act. He also has a moral power, in the exercise of which he can either heed or ignore its warnings.

Man is free in the sense of determining his own activities. This is proved by each man's own consciousness. A man is just as much aware of originating his own actions as he is of acting at all. Does he really act by his own power? Yes. And does he know that he acts by his own power? Yes. How does he know these things? He knows because he is conscious. His consciousness is the evidence of his being free.

Another aspect of man's moral state is that man can distinguish between the acts in which he is free and those in which he is acted upon by influences outside of his own choice. He knows that in some things he is a recipient of influences and of actions exerted upon himself, while in other things he is not a recipient in the same sense, but a voluntary actor. The fact that man can make this distinction proves that he is a free agent.

The difference to which I now refer is one of which everyone is well aware. Sometimes a man cannot tell from where his thoughts come. Impressions are made upon his mind, and he cannot trace the origin of them. They may be from above; they may be from beneath—he knows very little about their source, and little about them, except that they are not his own free volitions. Regarding the acts of his own will, there can be no such uncertainty. He knows their origin. He knows that they are the product of a power originating in himself, and he is compelled to hold himself primarily responsible for the exercise of them.

Not only does he have this direct consciousness, but as already suggested, he also has the testimony of his own conscience. This faculty, by its very nature, takes notice of his moral acts, requiring certain acts of will and forbidding others. This faculty is an essential condition of free moral agency. Possessing it, along with man's other mental powers, man must be free and under moral obligation.

It is inconceivable that man should be under moral law and government without the power of free moral action. The logical condition of the existence of a conscience in man is that he should be free.

That man is free is evident from the fact that he is conscious of praise or blameworthiness. He could not reasonably blame himself unless it were first true that he is free. This is a truth that no one can help knowing, however much he may desire to ignore it.

Just as conscience implies moral agency, so, where there is a conscience, it is impossible for men really to deny moral responsibility. Men can only blame themselves for wrongdoing. Knowing that their conscience has forewarned them against the wrong act, how can they evade the conviction that the act was wrong?

Again, the Bible always treats men as free agents, commanding them to do or not to do, as if they have all the power required to obey such commands. A young minister once said to me, "I preach that men ought to repent, but never that they can." "Why not also preach that they can?" I asked. He replied, "The Bible does not affirm that they can." To this I replied that it would be perfectly ridiculous for a human government to require certain duties but then to affirm that the people have no power to obey. The very requirement is the strongest possible affirmation that the people are able to do the things required. If the lawmakers did not believe this, how could they reasonably require obedience? The very first assumption to be made concerning good rulers is that they have common sense and common honesty. To deny that God has these qualities is blasphemous.

Freedom of will is one of the earliest convictions we have. Probably no one living can remember his first convictions of right and wrong. It is also one of our most irresistible convictions. We assume the freedom of our own will from the very beginning. The little child affirms it in his first efforts to accomplish his

God's Call

purposes. Look at him reaching forth to get his food
or his toys. His free will begins to act long before he
can understand it. He begins to act on his own responsibility, long before he can estimate what or
how great this responsibility is. The fact of personal
responsibility is fastened on us so that we can no
more escape this conviction than we can escape from
ourselves.

Human Beings Are in Moral Bondage

While it is undeniably true that men have this
attribute of moral liberty, it is equally true that they
are *morally enslaved*—they are in moral bondage.
They have liberty through their created makeup; the
bondage comes by voluntary perversion and abuse of
their powers.

The Bible portrays men as being in bondage—as
having the power to resist temptation to sin, yet as
voluntarily yielding to those temptations. The Bible
presents Satan as ruling the hearts of men at his
will. Satan ruled Eve in the Garden; now he *"works
in the sons of disobedience"* (Eph. 2:2).

What the Bible presents in regard to this matter, experience proves to be true. Wicked men know
that they are in bondage to Satan. Who do you think
puts it into the hearts of young people to plot iniquity and to drink it in like water? Is it not the Devil?
Many young men and women, when tempted, seem
to have no moral stamina to resist, but are swept
away by the first gust of temptation!

Human beings are in bondage to their appetites.
When their appetites are excited, they are led away
as Eve and Adam were. What can be the reason why

some young people find it so hard to give up the use of tobacco? They know the habit is filthy and disgusting; they know it must injure their health; but their appetites crave it, and the Devil encourages the craving. The poor victim makes a feeble effort to deliver himself, but the Devil turns the screw again and holds him tighter, and then drags him back to a harder bondage.

It is similar when a person is in bondage to alcohol, or any other form of fleshly indulgence. Satan urges the influence of this indulgence and does not care much what the particular form of it may be, provided its power is strong enough to ruin the soul. It all plays into his hand and promotes his main purpose.

Human beings are also in bondage to the love of money, the fashions of the world, and the opinions of other people. By these they are enslaved and led against the demands of duty. Everyone who is led counter to his convictions of duty is enslaved. He is free only when he acts in accordance with those convictions. This is the true idea of liberty. Only when reason and conscience control the will is a person free—for God made humans to be intelligent and moral beings who act under the influence of their own enlightened conscience and reason. This is the freedom that God exercises and enjoys; none can be higher or nobler. But when a moral agent is in bondage to his low appetites and passions, and is led by them to disregard the dictates of his conscience and of his reason, he is simply a slave to a very hard and cruel master.

God made people to be free, giving them all the mental powers that they need in order to control their own activities as a rational being would wish to. Their bondage, then, is altogether voluntary. They choose to resist the control of reason, and they submit to the control of appetite and passion.

Every impenitent individual is conscious of being in bondage to temptation. What man, if he is not saved from sin through grace, does not know that he is an enigma to himself? I would have little respect for any man who says he has never been ashamed of himself and has never found himself doing things he could not well account for. I would be especially ashamed—and afraid, too—if I were to hear a young man say he had never had a sense of his moral weakness. Such ignorance would only show his utter lack of reflection and his consequent failure to notice the most obvious moral phenomenon of his inner life. Does he not know that his weakest desires carry his will, despite the strongest convictions of his reason and conscience to the contrary?

To go against one's conscience in this way produces an entirely guilty state, because it is so altogether voluntary. It is greatly opposed to the convictions of one's reason and of one's understanding, and it is opposed to one's convictions of God's righteous demands. To go against such convictions, one must be supremely guilty.

Such conduct is most suicidal. The sinner acts in unquestioning opposition to his own best interests, so that if he has the power to ruin himself, this course of action will certainly do it. The course he pursues is, of all others, best adapted to destroy both body and soul. How, then, can it be anything but suicidal? The sinner actively denies all moral obligation; he knows the fact of his moral obligation, and yet he denies it in the face of his clearest convictions. How can this not be suicidal? Many times I have asked sinners how they could account for their own conduct. The honest ones answer, "I cannot at all; I am an enigma to myself." The real explanation is that, while they are free moral agents, they have sold themselves into moral bondage by the infatuation of sin, and they are really slaves to Satan and their own lusts.

This is a state of deep moral degradation. Intrinsically, it is highly disgraceful. Everybody feels that certain forms of sin and certain classes of sinners are disgraceful. We all feel that drunkenness is beastly. Think of the drunkard reeling about, mentally stupefied and reeking in his own filth! Is he not almost a beast? But not even a beast is so mean and so vile—no beast gives us such a sense of voluntary degradation. Compared with the self-besotted drunkard, any one of them is a noble creature.

We all say this, when we look only from our human standpoint. But there is another and better standpoint. How do angels look upon this self-made drunkard? They see him as only a little lower than themselves (Ps. 8:4–5), and as one who might have aspired to companionship with them, yet he chose instead to sink himself down to the level of swine! Oh, how their souls must recoil from the sight of such self-made degradation! To see the noble quality of intellect discarded, to see even nobler moral qualities disowned and trodden underfoot as if they were only an encumbrance—this is too much for angels to bear. Think of how they must feel!

But the drunkard is not alone in the contempt that his fleshly degradation entails. Consider one who smokes tobacco. The laws of the community exclude him from many places. Yet, for the sake of this low indulgence, the smoker is willing to go into indecent places. He will sneak out from among respectable people in order to herd with others who have the same filthy indulgence. If he were forced to spend the entire day in the society to which he sinks himself by this indulgence, it might warn him of the cost of his worldliness! It might help to open his eyes!

I have mentioned these forms of fleshly indulgence in order to illustrate the real degradation of sin. In these cases, the good sense of mankind has been shown by the degree of scorn that is cast upon these adherents of self-indulgence. If we only saw things in their right light, we would take the view of the so-called moralist. One popular "moralist" once said to me, "How can I act with regard to God or to what is right? How can I go to church with the high intention of pleasing God? I could go with a desire to promote my own selfish ends, but how can I go for the sake of pleasing God?"

Yes, this is precisely the sinner's difficulty and his guilt—he does not care how little he pleases God! That is the least of his concerns. The very lowest kind of motives sways his will and his life. He stands entirely apart from the reach of the highest and noblest intentions. In this we find his self-made degradation and his exceedingly great guilt.

This is true of the miser, when he gets beyond all motives but the love of hoarding—when his question is not "How will I honor the human race, bless my generation, or glorify my Maker?" but "How can I make a few more pennies?" Even when he is urged to pray, he will ask, "What profit will I have if I do pray to God?" When you find a man so incapable of being moved by noble influences, what a wretch he is! How indescribably base!

There is also the ambitious scholar, whose aims are too low to be influenced by the exalted motive of doing good, and who feels only what affects his reputation. Is this not exceedingly low and mean? What would you think of the preacher who lost all regard for the welfare of souls and thought only of maintaining his reputation? What would you say of him? You would declare that he was too mean and too wicked to live, and fit only for hell! What would you think of one who shines like Lucifer among the morning stars of intellect and genius, but who debases himself to the low and miserable activity of fishing for applause and compliments? Would you not say that such self-seeking is inexpressibly contemptible? With all heaven from above beckoning them on to lofty purposes and efforts, there they are, nosing after some little advantage to their small selves!

All this comes from bondage to selfishness. How unfortunate that there is so much of this in our world that public opinion rarely considers it according to its real nature!

REMARKS

1. Our subject reveals the case of those who are convicted of what is right but cannot be persuaded to do it. For example, a drunkard knows what his duty

is, knows he ought to reform, yet he will not change. Every sermon against alcohol carries conviction, but the next temptation sweeps it away, and he returns like the dog to his vomit (Prov. 26:11). But take note of this: every time temptation triumphs over the man's conviction that he should be sober, he is left weaker than before, and very soon you will find him utterly prostrate. Recall our text verse: *"By whom a person is overcome, by him also he is brought into bondage."* Miserable man! How certainly he will die in his sins!

No matter what the form of the temptation may be, he who is convinced of his duty, yet takes no corresponding action, is on the highway to perdition. Inevitably, this bondage grows stronger and stronger with every fresh trial of its strength. Every time you are convinced of your duty, and yet resist that conviction and refuse to act in accordance with it, you become more and more helpless; you commit yourself more and more to the control of your iron-hearted master. Every fresh case renders you only the more fully a helpless slave.

You may know of some young men or women who have already made themselves moral wrecks. There may be young people, not yet sixteen years old, who have already put their consciences beneath their feet and trampled on them. You young people, you have already learned to go against all your convictions of duty. How horrible! Every day your hands are growing stronger. With each day's resistance, your soul is more deeply and hopelessly lost. Poor miserable, dying sinner! *"He who is often rebuked, and hardens his neck, will suddenly be destroyed, and that without remedy"* (Prov. 29:1). Suddenly, you are thrown upon the breaking waves and are gone! Your friends move solemnly along the shore, looking out on the rocks of damnation on which your soul is wrecked. Weeping as they go, they mournfully say, "This is the destruction of one who knew his duty but did not do it. Thousands of times the appeals of conviction came to his heart, but he learned to resist them. He made it his business to resist, and unfortunately, he was only too successful!"

How insane the delusion, that the sinner's case is getting better while he is yet in his sins. The drunkard might as well imagine that he is getting better because every temperance lecture convicts him of his sin and shame, while every next day's temptation leaves him drunk as ever! Getting better! There can be no delusion as false and as fatal as this!

You can see the force of this delusion in clearer light when you notice how slight are the considerations that sway the soul against all the vast influences of God's character and kingdom. It must be a strong and fearful delusion that can make such tiny considerations outweigh such vast and momentous influences.

The guilt of this state can be estimated by the insignificance of the motives that control the mind. What would you think of the youth who could murder his father for only a dollar? "What!" you would exclaim. "To be bribed to murder his father for such a small pittance!" You would consider his guilt even greater by how much less the temptation is.

2. Our subject shows the need for the Holy Spirit to impress the truth on the hearts of sinners.

3. You may also see how certainly sinners will be lost if they grieve the Spirit of God away. Your

earthly friends might be discouraged, and yet you might be saved; but if the Spirit of God becomes discouraged and leaves you, your doom is sealed forever. *"Woe to them when I depart from them!"* (Hos. 9:12). This departure of God from the sinner gives the signal for tolling the bell for his lost soul. Then the mighty angel begins to toll the great bell of eternity: one more soul going to its eternal doom!

Nine

Men Often Look Highly upon What God Abhors

*You are those who justify yourselves before men,
but God knows your hearts. For what is highly esteemed
among men is an abomination in the sight of God.*
—Luke 16:15

C hrist spoke these words shortly after He had
given the parable of the unjust steward (Luke
16:1–8). Our Lord portrayed the steward as
being wise in the sense that he thought ahead and
was prudent, but his was a wisdom of the world,
empty of all morality. Christ used the case to rec-
ommend that we use wealth to make for ourselves
friends who, at our death, will welcome us into *"an
everlasting home"* (v. 9). Then, going to the bottom
principle that should control us in all our use of
wealth, He said that no man can serve both God and
money (v. 13). Rich and covetous men who are serving money need not suppose they can serve God at
the same time. The service of the one is not to be
reconciled with the service of the other.

The covetous Pharisees heard all these things
from Christ, and they derided Him. It was as if they
said, "Indeed, you seem to be very self-righteous, to
tell us that we do not acceptably serve God! When

has there ever been a tithe that we did not pay?" Those Pharisees did not acknowledge Christ's orthodoxy, by any means. They thought they could serve both God and money. They had nothing but scorn for the teachings that showed the inconsistency and absurdity of their worshiping two opposing gods and serving two opposing masters.

Our Lord replied to them with the words of our text verse: *"You are those who justify yourselves before men, but God knows your hearts. For what is highly esteemed among men is an abomination in the sight of God."* In discussing this subject, I will show how and why people look highly upon what God abhors.

Human beings have a high regard for what God hates because they have a different standard of judgment. God judges by one standard; they by another. God's standard requires universal benevolence; their standard is satisfied with any amount of selfishness, as long as it is sufficiently refined to meet the times. God requires men to devote themselves not to their own interests, but to His interests and those of His great family. He establishes one great end of all things—the highest glory of His name and kingdom. He asks them to become divinely patriotic, devoting themselves to their Creator and to the good of His creatures.

The world adopts an entirely different standard, allowing men to establish their own happiness as their end. It is interesting that some so-called philosophers have laid down the same standard: that men should pursue their own happiness supremely, and only take care not to infringe on others' happiness too much. Their doctrine allows men to pursue a selfish course, only not in a way to infringe too obviously on others' rights and interests.

But God's standard is, "Do not seek your own." (See 1 Corinthians 10:24.) His law is explicit: *"You shall love* [not yourself, but] *the LORD your God with all your heart"* (Deut. 6:5). *"Love is the fulfillment of the law"* (Rom. 13:10). *"Love* [this same love]...*does not seek its own"* (1 Cor. 13:4–5). This is characteristic of the love that the law of God requires—it does not seek its own. *"Let no one seek his own, but each one the other's well-being"* (1 Cor. 10:24). *"Let each of you look out not only for his own interests, but also for the interests of others"* (Phil. 2:4). *"For all seek their own, not the things which are of Christ Jesus"* (v. 21). To seek their own interests and not Jesus Christ's, Paul regarded as an entire departure from the standard of true Christianity.

In God's eyes, nothing is virtue except devotion to Christ's interests. The right goal is the general good, not one's own. Hence God's standard requires virtue, while man's standard at best only restrains vice. All human governments are based on this principle. They do not require benevolence; they only restrain selfishness. In the foundation principles of our government, it is affirmed that men have certain inalienable rights, one of which is the right to pursue happiness. This is affirmed to be an inalienable right, and it is always assumed to be right in itself, provided that it does not infringe on others' rights or happiness. But God's standard requires benevolence and regards nothing else as virtue except devotion to the highest good. Man's standard condemns nothing, provided that man so restrains himself as not to infringe on others' rights.

Men very inconsiderately judge themselves and others, not by God's standard, but by man's. They do this to an amazing extent. Look into men's real opinions, and you will see this. Often, without being at all aware of it, men judge themselves, not by God's standard, but by their own.

Here I must point out some of the proof of this, and furnish some illustrations.

Suppose, for example, that a man lives in a community and does no harm, defrauds no man, does not cheat or lie, does no perceptible injury to society, and transacts his business in a way deemed highly honorable and virtuous. This man stands in high repute according to the standard of the world. But what does all this really amount to? The man is just taking care of himself; that is all. His morality is merely neutral. All you can say of him is, "He does no harm." Yet this morality is often spoken of in a manner that shows that the world holds it in high regard. But does God look highly upon it? No; it is abomination in His sight!

As another example, a religion that is merely neutral is often highly esteemed by the world. People of this type of religion are careful not to do wrong, but what is doing wrong? It is thought to be no wrong to neglect the souls of their neighbors. What do they consider wrong? Cheating, lying, stealing—these and similar things they will admit are wrong. But what are they doing? Look around you, and you will see what these people are doing. Many of them never try to save a soul. They are regarded highly for their inoffensive lives. They do no wrong, but they do nothing to save a soul. Their religion is a mere negation. Perhaps they will not go to work on Sunday, but they would never save a soul from death. They would let their own employees go to hell without one earnest effort to save them. Must not such a religion be an abomination to God?

It is the same for a religion that, at best, consists of forms and prayers and does not contain the energies of benevolent effort. Such a religion is all hollow. Is it serving God to do nothing but ask favors for oneself?

Some people keep up their Sunday duties and family prayer, but all their religion consists in keeping up their forms of worship. If they add nothing to these, their religion is only an abomination before God.

Still other facts show that men loosely set up a false standard, which they highly esteem, but which God abhors. For example, they will require true religion only of ministers, but no real religion of anybody else. All men agree that ministers should be really pious. These people also require ministers to be benevolent and to be involved in ministry for the high purpose of doing good, not for the mere sake of making a living. Nothing these ministers do can be for the sake of monetary gain, but only for the sake of souls and out of unselfish love. Otherwise, people will have no confidence in a minister.

But turn this around and apply it to people in business. Do they judge themselves by this rule? Do they judge each other by this rule? Before people will have Christian confidence in a salesperson or a mechanic, do they insist that these individuals should be as much above greed as a minister should be? Should they be as willing as a minister to give up their time to the sick—be as ready to forego a better salary for the sake of doing more good, as they insist a minister should be? No, businesspeople are never required to have the kind of Christian character that is required of Gospel ministers.

A businessman may do a service for you, write out his bill, and collect the money from you. Now, suppose I go and visit a sick man to give him spiritual counsel. I may visit him from time to time, for counsel and for prayer, until he dies, and then I attend his funeral. Having done this service, if I were to write up my bill and send it to his family, would there not be some talk? People would say, "What right has he to do that? He ought to perform that service for the love of souls, and not charge for it."

Consider how this applies to the ministers who are not being paid a salary to perform this service, of whom there are many. If any one of these men goes and labors among the sick or at funerals, he must not take pay. But if one of these ministers wishes to have his saw sharpened, he must pay for it. He may send it to the same man whose sick family he has visited by day and by night, and whose dead he has buried without charge—"for the love of souls." But no such "love of souls" is required of the mechanic in his service. The truth is, what is considered religion in a layman is considered *sin* in a minister. I do not complain that men take pay for labor, but that they do not apply the same standards to a minister.

The aims and practices of businesspeople are almost universally an abomination in the sight of God. Almost all of these are based on the same principle as human governments are, namely, that the only restraints imposed will be to prevent men from being too selfish. Men are thus allowed to be just as selfish as they can be as long as others have an equal chance to be selfish.

I could enumerate the principles of businesspeople regarding their objectives and modes of doing business. But what would it all amount to? Seeking their own ends; doing something for themselves, not for others. As long as they do it in a way regarded as honest and honorable among men, no further restriction is imposed upon them.

Take a Bible society as an illustration of this point. This institution is not for the good and profit of those who publish Bibles. Rather, the objective is to furnish Bibles as cheaply to the purchaser as possible, so as to put a Bible into the hands of every human being at the lowest possible price. Now, it is easy to see that any other course and any different principle from this would be universally condemned. If Bible societies were to become merely for profit, they would cease to be benevolent institutions at all, and this would bring down on them the curses of men. But all business ought to be done as benevolently as the making of Bibles; why not? If it is not benevolent, how can it have the approval of God? What is a benevolent business? It is that which is undertaken for the doing of the utmost good. In this sense, men ought to be devoted and benevolent, and they should focus their attention on giving God the glory in all they do, whether they eat or drink or whatever they may do. (See 1 Corinthians 10:31.)

Yet where do you find the individual who holds his fellowmen to this standard before he will regard them highly as Christians? Who requires all men, in all their business, to be as benevolent as Bible societies are? What would we say of a Bible society that gets as much as it can for its Bibles, instead of selling at the lowest price? What would you say of such a Bible society? You would say, "Horrible hypocrites!" I must say the same of every Christian who does the same thing. As for ungodly men, they do not profess any Christian benevolence, so we cannot charge this hypocrisy on them. But we will try to get this light before their minds.

Now think of a minister and ask yourself, "Do I judge myself as I judge him?" Do you say of yourself, "I ought to do for others, without compensation, all that I require him to do without compensation"?

Apply this to all businesspeople. No matter what your business is—whether small or great, whether sharpening saws or banking—you call the Bible society benevolent. Do you make your business as much and as truly benevolent as the Bible society? If not, why not? What right have you to be less benevolent than those who print, publish, and sell Bibles?

Selfish ambition is another thing that is highly esteemed among men, yet is an abomination before God. How often we see this regarded highly! I have been amazed to see how people form judgments on this matter. Consider a young man who is a good student, who is making great progress in his studies. Such young people are often spoken of in the highest terms. Provided they do well for themselves, nothing more seems to be asked or expected in order to entitle them to high praise. This is a thing the Devil might do.

I recall the case of a lawyer who was greatly esteemed by his fellowmen. He was often spoken of well by Christians, but what was he? Nothing but an ambitious young lawyer, doing everything for ambition—and for what? To get some good for himself. Yet he is sought out by Christian families! Why? Because he is doing well for himself.

The world's entire morality, and that of a large portion of the church, is only a false benevolence. You may see a family very much united and you say, "How they love one another!" And so they do, but they may be very exclusive. They may shut off their sympathies almost utterly from all other families, and they may consequently exclude themselves from doing good in the world. The same kind of morality may be seen in towns and in nations. This makes up the entire morality of the world.

Many people have what they call humanitarianism, without any piety, and this is often highly esteemed among men. They pretend to love others, but after all, they do not honor God or even aim at honoring Him. In their love of mankind, they fall below some animals. I doubt whether many impious men and women would do what I once knew a dog to do. Its master wanted to kill it, and so he took the dog out into the river in a boat and tied a stone around its neck. In the struggle to throw dog and stone overboard together, the boat was upset. The man was then in the river, and the dog, after struggling to release the stone from its neck, seized its master by the collar and swam with him to land. Few people would have had enough benevolence— even without piety—to have done this. Indeed, men without piety are not often half as kind to each other as animals are. Men are more degraded and more depraved. Animals will make greater sacrifices for each other than the human race will. Whales will allow themselves to be murdered to protect a school of their young. Yet many human mothers think they do the most admirable things because they take care of their children.

But people ought to act with higher intentions than animals do. If they do not, they act wickedly. Knowing more than animals can know—having the knowledge of God and of the dying Savior as their example and standard—human beings, therefore, have higher responsibilities than animals can have.

From this, you can see that all those so-called religious efforts that men make, having only self for their end, are an abomination to God. I abhor a piety that has no benevolence in it, as deeply as I condemn its opposite—benevolence without piety. God loves both piety and benevolence. How greatly, then, must He abhor one when it is unnaturally divorced from the other!

Suppose there is a wealthy man who agrees to give $2000 toward building a splendid church. He thinks this is a very benevolent offering and that it may be highly esteemed among his fellowmen. But before God approves of it, He will look into the motives of the giver—and so may we, if we please. We find that this man owns a good deal of real estate in the village, which he expects will increase in value on the same day that the site of the church building is decided upon—enough to put back into his pocket two- or threefold what he has paid out. Besides this, he has other motives. He thinks of the increased respectability of having a fine place of worship—and of having the best seat in it for himself. Furthermore, he has some interest in having good morals sustained in the village, for vice is troublesome and somewhat dangerous to rich men. And then he has an indefinable sort of expectation that this new church and his handsome donation to build it will somehow improve his prospects for heaven. Although his prospects are rather dim at best, the improvement, though indefinite, is certainly one of his objectives. Now, if you look at these motives carefully, you will see that from first to last they are altogether selfish. Of course they are an abomination in God's sight!

The motives for getting a popular minister are often of the same sort. The objective is not to get a man sent by God, to labor for God and with God, and one with whom the people may labor and pray for souls and for God's kingdom. Rather, the people desire something else than this, and it is an abomination before God.

The highest forms of the world's morality are only abominations in God's sight. The world has what it calls good husbands, good wives, good children—but what sort of goodness is this? The husband loves his wife and seeks to please her. She also loves and seeks to please him. But do either of them love or seek to please God in these relationships? By no means. Nothing can be further from their thoughts. They never go beyond the narrow circle of self. Take all these human relationships in their best earthly form, and you will find that they never rise above the morality of the lowest animals. They pamper and caress each other, and they seem to take some interest in the care of their children. But so do the hens in your chicken coop—perhaps even more so. Often these fowls go beyond the world's morality in the qualities that the world calls *good*.

Should not human beings have vastly higher aims than these? Can God deem their highly esteemed qualities as anything other than an abomination if in fact they are below the level of domestic animals?

An unsanctified education falls into the same category. A good education is indeed a great benefit, but if it is not sanctified, if it is not used for God, it is all the more abominable to God. Yes, to the extent that you understand your duty and yet sin against the light that you have, it is only more abominable to Him. The same accomplishments that will give you higher regard among men will, if unsanctified, make your character more utterly abominable before God. You may be a polished writer and a beautiful speaker. You may stand at the head of the college in these respects. Your friends may look forward to the time when you will move audiences to admiration by your eloquence. But you have no piety!

When we ask, "How does God look upon such unsanctified talents?" we are compelled to answer, "Only as an abomination." The eloquent young student is only the more abominable to God because of all his unsanctified abilities. The very things that give you more honor among men will make you only the scoff of hell. The spirits of the abyss will meet you as they did the fallen monarch of Babylon, tauntingly saying, "Why are you here? You who could shake kingdoms by your eloquence, have you been brought down to the sides of the pit? You who might have been an angel of light—you, a selfish, doomed sinner—away and be out of our company! We have nobody here so guilty and so deeply damned as you!" (See Isaiah 14:4, 9–17.)

The same is true of all unsanctified talents—beauty, education, accomplishments—all, if unsanctified, are an abomination in the sight of God. All of those things that might make you more useful in the sight of God, if misused, are only the greater abomination in His sight.

A legalistic religion, with which you serve God only because you must, is also an abomination before God. You go to church, yet not out of love for God or for His worship, but out of regard for your reputation, your hope, or your conscience. Must not such a religion be, of all things, most abominable to God?

REMARKS

The world has mainly lost the true idea of religion. This is too obvious from all I have said to need more illustration. To a great extent, the same is true of the church. Professing Christians judge themselves falsely because they judge by a false standard.

One of the most common and fatal mistakes is to use a merely neutral standard. By this I mean that people take no action. Some people complain that they have a lack of conviction. Why don't they take the right standard and judge themselves by that? Suppose you had let a house burn down and made no effort to save it; what would you think of the guilt of stupidity and laziness there? Two women and five children were burnt to ashes in the fire; why didn't you give the alarm when you saw the fire taking hold? Why didn't you rush into the building and drag out the unconscious residents? Oh, you felt sluggish that morning—just as people talk of being "sluggish" in religion! Well, you hope not to be judged very hard, since you did not set the house on fire; you only let it alone; all you did was to do *nothing!*

This is what many people plead regarding their religious duties. They do nothing to pluck sinners out of the fire, and they seem to think this is a very valuable religion! Was this the religion of Jesus Christ or of Paul? Is it the religion of real benevolence, or even of common sense?

Many people who have a Christian hope indulge it on merely neutral grounds. Often I ask people how they are getting along in religion. They answer, "Pretty well," and yet they are doing nothing that is really religious. They are making no effort to save souls, are doing nothing to serve God. What are they doing? Oh, they keep up the forms of prayer! Suppose you were to hire an employee and pay him each week, yet he does nothing all day long but pray to you!

Religion is very easily understood. It is warfare. What does a warrior do? He devotes himself to the service of his country. If need be, he lays down his life on her altar. He is expected to do this. The same is true when a man is to lay down his life on God's altar, to be used in life or death, as God may please, in His service.

As this chapter has made clear, the things most highly regarded among men are often the very things God most abhors. Take, for example, the legalist's religion. The more earnestly he groans under his bondage to sin, the more the world esteems and

God abhors his religion. People will say of him, "The good man was all his life *'subject to bondage'* (Heb. 2:15)! He was in doubt and fear all his life!" But why did he not come by faith into that liberty with which Christ makes His people free (Gal. 5:1)?

A morality based on the most refined selfishness stands in the highest esteem among men, but God abhors it. People may say, "He was such a good man, almost a saint," yet God will hold him in utter abomination.

In the world's eyes, the good Christian is never abrupt, never aggressive, yet he is greatly admired. He has a selfish devotion to pleasing men, and nothing is more admired than this. I heard of a minister who did not have an enemy in the world. He was said to be most like Christ among all the men they knew. I thought it strange that a man so like Christ should have no enemies, for Christ had a great many enemies, and very bitter enemies, too. Indeed, it is said, *"All who desire to live godly in Christ Jesus will suffer persecution"* (2 Tim. 3:12). But when I came to learn the facts of the case, I understood the man. He never allowed himself to preach anything that could displease even Universalists. In fact, he had two Universalists among his elders. He also had some Calvinists, and he could by no means displease them. His motto was, "Please the people"—nothing but this. In the midst of a revival, he would leave the meetings and go to a party. Why? To please the people.

Now, this may be highly esteemed among men, but doesn't God abhor it? Absolutely!

It is a trivial thing to be judged by man's judgment, and all the more trivial since man is so prone to judge by a false standard. What is it to me that my fellowmen condemn me when God approves? The longer I live, the less I think of human opinions on the great questions of right and wrong as God sees them. People will judge both themselves and others falsely. Even the church sometimes condemns and excommunicates her best people. I could name cases in which I am confident this very thing was done. People have been cut off from communion in the church, and now everybody sees that those who were excommunicated were the best members of the church.

It is a blessed thought that the only thing we need to care for is to please God. The only question we need to ask is, "What will God think of it?" We have only One to please, and that is the Great Mind of the universe. If this is our single aim, we will not fail to please Him. But if we do not aim for this, everything we do is only an abomination in His sight.

Ten

Death to Sin through Christ

Likewise you also, reckon yourselves to be dead indeed to sin, but alive to God in Christ Jesus our Lord.
—Romans 6:11

The context of this passage will help us to understand its meaning. Near the end of the previous chapter in Romans, Paul had said,

> *The law entered that the offense might abound. But where sin abounded, grace abounded much more, so that as sin reigned in death, even so grace might reign through righteousness to eternal life through Jesus Christ our Lord.* (Rom. 5:20–21)

Here he spoke of sin as being a reigning principle, and of grace also as reigning. Then, in chapter six, he went on to say,

> *What shall we say then? Shall we continue in sin that grace may abound?...Likewise you also, reckon yourselves to be dead indeed to sin, but alive to God in Christ Jesus our Lord.* (Rom. 6:1, 11)

In these verses, Paul spoke of the old sinner as being crucified with Christ—so destroyed by the

moral power of the Cross that he who was once a
sinner will no longer serve sin. The language used
here seems to indicate that our death to sin is precisely analogous to Christ's death for sin. But this is
not the case. We are dead to sin in the sense that it
is no longer to be our master, implying that it has
been in power over us. But sin was never in power
over Jesus Christ, was never His master. Christ died
to abolish its power over us, not to abolish any power
of sin over Himself, for it had none. The analogy
goes to this extent and no further: He died for the
sake of making an atonement for sin and of creating
a moral power that could kill the love of sin in all
hearts; but the Christian dies to sin in the sense of
being divorced from all sympathy with sin and being
emancipated from its control.

But now I will examine the text verse in greater
depth, and in doing so, I will answer the following
questions:

1. What is it to be dead to sin in the sense of the
   text?
2. What is it to be alive to God?
3. What is it to reckon ourselves to be dead to sin?
4. What is it reckon ourselves to be alive to God
   through Jesus Christ?
5. What is implied in the exhortation of our text?

Dead to Sin

First, what does it mean to be dead to sin in the
sense of the text? Being dead to sin is obviously the
opposite of being dead in sin. The latter is undeniably
a state of entire sinfulness—a state in which the soul

is dead to all good through the power of sin over it. On the other hand, to be dead *to* sin is to be indifferent to its attractions, beyond the reach of its influences, and as fully removed from its influences as the dead are from the world. As he who is dead in the natural sense has nothing more to do with earthly things, so he who is dead to sin no longer has anything to do with sin's attractions or with sinning itself.

Alive to God

Second, what is it to be alive to God? It is to be full of life for Him, to be altogether active and on the alert to do His will. It is to make our whole lives a perpetual offering to Him, constantly delivering ourselves up to Him and His service, so that we may glorify His name and carry out His interests.

Believing That You Are Dead to Sin

Third, what is it to *"reckon"* ourselves *"dead indeed to sin"*? The word translated as *"reckon"* is sometimes rendered *account*. Abraham's faith was accounted unto him for righteousness (Rom. 4:9). Similarly, in this passage, *"reckon"* must mean *believe, consider* yourselves dead indeed unto sin. Account this to be the case. Regard this as your true relationship to sin. You are entirely dead to it; it will have no more dominion over you.

A careful examination of the passages where this original word is used will show that this is its usual and natural sense. And this gives us the true idea of Gospel faith—personally embracing the salvation that is by faith in Jesus Christ.

Alive through Jesus Christ

What is meant by reckoning yourselves alive indeed to God through Jesus Christ? Plainly this: you are to expect to be saved by Jesus Christ and to consider this salvation your own. You are to consider yourself as wholly dead to sin and as consequently brought into life and peace in Christ Jesus.

The Implications of This Exhortation

Now, the exhortation of our text implies that there is adequate provision for this expectation and for making these blessings real to you. For if there were no grounds for making them real, the command would be most absurd. A precept requiring us to consider ourselves *"dead indeed to sin, but alive to God"* would be utterly impossible if no provision were made for us to have such relationships to sin on the one hand, and to God through Christ on the other. If these blessings could not be reasonably expected, there could be no rational grounds for the expectation. If it were not reasonable to expect it, then to command us to expect it would be entirely unreasonable. Who does not see that the very command implies that there is a foundation laid and adequate provision made for the state required?

In complying with this command, the following things are implied.

First, it is implied that we believe that such a thing is possible. We believe that it is possible that, through Christ, we may live in the required manner, that we may avoid sin, give it up and abandon it altogether, and put it away forever. One cannot knowingly comply with this precept unless he also believes in its feasibility—a state actually made feasible by adequate grace, adapted to the laws of the mind and to the actual moral condition of lost men.

Second, it is implied that we cease from all expectation of attaining this state by our own independent, unaided efforts. We cannot begin to receive by grace until we renounce all expectation of attaining by natural works. It is only when we are empty of self that we begin to be filled with Christ.

Third, a present willingness to be saved from sin is also implied. We must actually renounce all sin because it is sin. The mind must take this position: "I can have nothing more to do with sinning, for God hates sin, and I am to live henceforth and forever to please and glorify Him. My soul is committed with its utmost strength of purpose to pleasing God and doing His will."

Fourth, it also implies an entire committal of your case to Jesus Christ, not only for present salvation from sin, but also for all future salvation from it. This is absolutely essential. It must always be the vital step, the cardinal act in this great work of salvation from sin.

Fifth, it also implies the closing of the mind against temptation, in such a sense that the mind truly expects to live a life purely devoted to God. This is the same sort of closing of the mind that takes place under a faithful marriage contract. When two people are solemnly betrothed in mutual, honest fidelity, there is no longer any thought of letting the eye wander or the heart go abroad for a fresh object of interest and love. The heart is fixed—willingly and by faith—and this fact shuts out the power of temptation almost entirely. It makes it a comparatively easy matter to keep the heart safely above the influence of temptation. Before the sacred vows are taken, individuals may be excused for looking around and making any observations or inquiries—but never after the solemn vow is made. After the parties have become one by vow of marriage, never to be broken, there is to be no more question as to a better choice—no further thought about changing the relationship or withdrawing the heart's affections. No wavering is admissible now; the pledge is made for everlasting faithfulness, settled once and forever!

This illustration is prominent in the Bible. Christians are represented as the bride of Christ. (See John 3:29.) Their relationship to Him is closely analogous to that of a bride to her husband. Hence when Christians commit their whole hearts to Him, resting their affections in Him and trusting Him for all good, their hearts are strongly closed against temptation.

This is God's own illustration, and surely no other would be more suitable or powerful. It shows how the Christian should view sin and all temptation to sin. He must say, "Away from my heart forever! I am married to Jesus Christ; how can I look for other lovers? My mind is forever settled. My affections are fixed—to wander no more! I can think of yielding to sin's seductions no longer. I cannot entertain the question for a moment. I can have nothing to do with sinning. My mind is settled; the question is forever closed. I can no more entertain the temptation to small sins than to great sins, can no more consent to give my heart to worldly idols than to commit murder! I did not enter into religion as an experiment, to see how I might like it—no more than a loyal husband and wife treat the marriage vow as an experiment. No; my whole soul has committed itself to Jesus Christ with as much expectation of being faithful forever as the most faithful husband and wife have of fulfilling their vows in all fidelity until death shall part them."

Christians in this state of mind no more expect to commit small sins than great sins. Since they hate all sin for its own sake and for its hatefulness to Christ, any sin, however small, is to them like murder. Thus, if the heart is ever afterward seduced and overcome by temptation, it is altogether contrary to their expectation and purpose. It was not part of their plan by any means, but was distinctly excluded. The temptation broke on them unexpectedly, perhaps because of old habits or associations.

Sixth, the state of mind in question implies that the Christian knows where his great strength lies. He knows it does not lie in works of fasting, giving to charity, saying prayers, doing public or private duties—nothing of this sort, not even in resolutions or any self-originated efforts, but only in Christ received by faith. He no more expects spiritual life apart from Christ than a sane man would expect to fly by swinging his arms in the air. Deep in his soul lies the conviction that his whole strength lies in Christ alone.

When a person is so enlightened that he truly understands this subject, then to expect less than this from Jesus Christ as the result of committing the whole soul to Him for full salvation is virtually to reject Him as a revealed Savior. It does not honor

211

Him for what He is; it does not honor the revelations He has made of Himself in His Word by accepting Him as He is presented there. Consider that the first element of this salvation is not being saved from hell, but being saved from sin. Salvation from punishment is a secondary thing. It is only a result of being saved from sin, and it is not the primary element in the Gospel salvation. Why was the infant Messiah to be called Jesus? Because *"He will save His people from their sins"* (Matt. 1:21). Does the Bible teach any other view than this?

REMARKS

1. Our text verse alone, *"Likewise you also, reckon yourselves to be dead indeed to sin, but alive to God in Christ Jesus,"* entirely justifies the expectation of living without sin through all-abounding grace. If there were no other passage concerning this point, this alone would be adequate. If a Christian offers this as the only reason for his hope in Christ, he offers as good a reason as he needs to give. Even so, there are indeed many other Scripture passages that fully justify this expectation.

2. To teach that such an expectation is a dangerous error is to teach unbelief. What if the apostle had added to this command—which requires us to account ourselves *"dead indeed to sin, but alive to God"*—the following statement: "Yet let me warn you; nobody can rationally hope to be free from sin in this world. You must remember that to entertain such an expectation as God commands in these

words is a dangerous error." What would be thought of this if it were attached to Romans 6:11?

No man can deny that the passage speaks of sanctification, of being holy before God. The whole question is, Will Christians *"continue in sin"* (Rom. 6:1) after having been forgiven and accepted by their Redeemer? Paul labored to show that they may die to sin, even as Christ died for sin. He also explained that they may live a new, spiritual life, through faith in His grace, even as Christ lives a higher and more glorious life.

Here let me refer to another passage:

> *Do not be unequally yoked together with unbelievers. For...what agreement has the temple of God with idols? For you are the temple of the living God....Therefore "Come out from among them and be separate, says the Lord. Do not touch what is unclean, and I will receive you." "I will be a Father to you, and you shall be My sons and daughters, says the LORD Almighty."*
>
> *(2 Cor. 6:14, 16–18)*

> *Therefore, having these promises, beloved, let us cleanse ourselves from all filthiness of the flesh and spirit, perfecting holiness in the fear of God.* *(2 Cor. 7:1)*

These verses are part of a very remarkable passage. Note how precept and promise are intermingled, and how the precept admonishing us to perfect holiness is founded on the basis of a most glorious promise. Now, what would we think of Paul, and of the divine Spirit who spoke through Paul, if he had immediately added, "Take care, lest any of you should be led by these remarks to indulge the very dangerous and erroneous expectation that you can 'perfect holiness,' or cleanse yourselves from any sin, either of flesh or spirit, in this world"? Would this not have been trifling with the intelligence and Christian sensitivity of every reader of Paul's words throughout all time? Should we not consider it as substantially blasphemous?

It so happens that the Bible never contradicts its own teachings. But what if it had? What if the Bible had solemnly asserted, "No mere man, either of himself or by any grace received in this life, has ever wholly kept or shall ever keep the commandments of God, but he daily breaks them in thought, word, and deed"?

To teach that such an expectation is dangerous is a great deal worse than no teaching at all. It would be far better to leave men to their own unaided reading of God's Word, for then they would not be so sadly misled, no matter how inclined they might be to the misunderstanding. How can it be dangerous to expect salvation from sin? Dangerous? What does this mean? Is it dangerous to expect victory over any sin? If so, what is the Gospel worth? What Gospel do we have that can be deemed Good News at all?

Many people indulge the very opposite expectation. Far from expecting anything like what Paul authorized them to expect, they know they have no expectation to live without sin through grace. Others expect to be always in sin. They depend on reckoning themselves not *"dead indeed to sin,"* but somewhat alive to it all their lives, and somewhat alive to God through Jesus Christ.

214

Anyone who has been wounded and made sore by sin—its bitter darts sinking deep into his moral being—anyone who has known its bitterness and felt its poison drink up his spirit will see that there is glory in the idea of being delivered from sin. He will surely see that this deliverance is by far the greatest need of his soul, and that nothing can be compared with escaping from this *"body of sin"* (Rom. 6:6) and death. Look at Romans 7. There you will see the state of a man who is more than convinced—he is really convicted. It is one thing to be convinced, but to be convicted shows greater progress in the right direction. This term *convicted* implies the intervention of another party. The criminal before the judge may be quite convinced of his guilt, but his being convicted is a still further step; the testimony and the jury convict him.

Some of you know what it is to see yourself as a sinner, and yet seeing this fact brings with it no sting; it does not cut deep into your soul. On the other hand, some of you may know what it is to see your sins piercing you through and through with daggers. Then you cry out, *"O wretched man that I am! Who will deliver me from this body of death?"* (Rom. 7:24). You feel a piercing sting, as if your soul were filled with poison—with dark, rankling venom, pouring out through the depths of your soul the very agonies of hell! This is what I mean by being convicted, as a state of mind beyond being merely convinced. The daggers and the smiting of sin seem really like the piercings of an arrow, as if arrows from the Almighty really did drink up your spirit. (See Job 6:4.) When you experience this, then you can understand what the Good News of the Gospel is. A remedy for such pangs is most certainly good news! To know that the blood of Christ can save is indeed life to the fainting soul.

Suppose a man is in this state of cutting, piercing conviction, and feels that there is no remedy. He sinks under the iron spears of despair. See his agony! Tell him there can never be any remedy for his guilty soul! Say to him, "You must lie there in your despair forever!" Can any state of mind be more horrible?

I remember a case that occurred in Reading, Pennsylvania, many years ago. There was a man of hard heart and iron frame, a strong, burly man who had stood up against the revival in that city as if he could shake off all *"the arrows of the Almighty"* (Job 6:4). But he had a praying wife and a praying sister, and they gathered in prayer around him. Soon it was apparent that an arrow from the quiver of the Almighty had pierced between the joints of his armor and had taken hold of his innermost heart. Oh, he was in agony then!

It was a dark and intensely cold night. It seemed that he absolutely could not live. They sent for me to come and see him. I went. While still about sixty feet from his house, I heard his screams of woe. It made me feel awfully solemn—his wails were so like the echoes of the pit of hell! When I reached the house, there he lay on the floor, rolling in his agony and wailing, such as is rarely heard this side the pit of despair. Cold as the weather was, his sweat was falling from him like rain, with his entire body intensely perspiring. Oh, his groans! To see him gnaw on his tongue—this could not help but give one some idea of the doom of the damned! "Oh," I said, "if this is only conviction, what is hell?"

But the man could not bear to hear anything about sin. His conscience was already full of it; the awful things of God's law had already been brought to his attention, so that nothing more was left to be done in that direction. I could only put Christ before him, and just hold his mind to focusing on Christ alone. This soon brought relief. But suppose I had nothing else to say but, "Mr. B——, there is no help possible for your case! You can wail on and on; no being in the universe can help you." Would he have believed it if I had told him that hell has no fire? He had enough fire in his burning soul already! It seemed to him that no hell of fire could possibly be worse than this.

How perfectly horrible for people to oppose the idea of expecting deliverance from sin and yet talk calmly of going on in sin all the rest of their earthly days! An elder whom I knew rose once in a church meeting and told the Lord he had been living in sin thus far, so he expected to go on in sin as long as he lived. He had sinned today, so he would undoubtedly sin tomorrow and so on. Yet he talked as calmly about it all as if it were foolish to make any ado, as well as impossible to attempt any change for the better. To talk of this calmly—think of that! To talk calmly of living in sin all the rest of his days! How horrible! Suppose a wife should say to her husband, "I love you some, but you know I love many other men, too, and that I find it pleasant to indulge myself with them. You certainly must be aware that all women are frail creatures and are liable to fall continually. Indeed, you know that I expect to fall more or less every day that I live, so you certainly cannot expect from me anything so impossible and fanatical as unblemished virtue! You know that none of us has any idea of being perfect in the present life—we don't believe in any such thing!"

Now let me ask you to look at this woman and hear what she has to say. Can you hear her talk so, without having your soul filled with horror? This woman, a wife, yet she thinks and talks in this way about marital fidelity!

And yet this is not so different from the case of the Christian who says, "I expect to sin every day I live," and who says this carelessly and without emotion. You expect to be a traitor to Jesus each day of your life; to crucify Him afresh each day (Heb. 6:6 KJV); to put Him each day to open shame; each day to dishonor His name, grieve His heart, and bring sorrow and shame upon all who love Christ's cause; and yet you talk about having a good hope through grace! But tell me, does not every true Christian say, "Do not let me live at all if I cannot live without sin, for how can I bear to go on day by day sinning against Him whom I love so much?"

Those who are really opposed to this idea are either very ignorant of what the Gospel is, or they are impenitent and of course do not care to be delivered from their sins. Or, at best, they are guilty of great unbelief. Into which of these classes the opposers of the doctrine may fall is a question for themselves to settle, between their own consciences and their God.

3. There are two distinct views of salvation entertained by professing Christians. Correspondingly, there are two distinct classes of believers, often within the same church. The one class of believers sees the Gospel as a salvation from sin. They think

more of this aspect of the Gospel and value it more than the hope of heaven or of earth. The great thing with them is to realize the idea of deliverance from sin. This is the charm and glory of the Gospel. They seek freedom from sin more than to be saved from hell. They care more to be saved from sin itself than from its consequences. They think and pray very little about the consequences of sin. It is their glory and their joy that Christ was sent to deliver them from their bondage in iniquity, to lift them up from their wretched state and give them the liberty of love. This they labor to realize; this is to them the Good News of Gospel salvation.

Believers in the other class are mostly anxious to be saved from hell. The punishment due for sin is the thing they chiefly fear. In fact, fear has been mainly the reason for their religious efforts. The Gospel is not thought of as a means of deliverance from sin, but as a great system that takes away the fear and danger of damnation, though it leaves them still in their sin. They seem not to notice that a scheme of salvation that removes the fear of damnation for sin, that leaves them still in their sins to live for themselves, and that maintains the belief that Christ will in the end bring them to heaven (despite their having lived in sin all their days), is a compromise on a most magnificent scale. By virtue of it, the whole church is expected to wallow on in sin through life, and be no less sure of heaven in the end.

You will find these opposing views everywhere as you go among the churches. Many people in the church are altogether worldly and selfish; they live conformed to the world and negligent of their duties.

They expect to indulge themselves in sin throughout their lives. You may ask them, "Do you think this is right?" They will answer, "No." "Why, then, do you do it?" "Oh, we are all imperfect, and we can't expect to be any better than imperfect while here in the flesh." Yet they expect to be saved from hell in the end and to have all their sins forgiven. But how? Not by sincerely turning away from all their sins, but on the assumption that the Gospel is a vast system of indulgences—more vast by far than Pope Leo X ever used to comfort sinners in his day. For these people are not merely those who sin occasionally, but those who live in sin and know they do; these people expect that they will sin as long as they live, yet they expect to be saved in the end.

The first class of professing Christians have no expectation of being saved unless they have pure hearts and live above the world. Talk to them about living in sin; they hate and dread the very thought. To them, it is poison. Sin is bitter to their souls. They dread it as they dread death itself. Believers in this class are in agony if they find themselves even slipping, and they are especially cautious against exposing themselves to temptation. The real Christian may be known by this, that the very thought of being drawn into sin drives him to agony. He cannot bear the idea of living in sin; no, not for one moment.

It is not so with the latter class. Suppose a wife should say to her husband, "I am determined to go to the theater." "But, my dear," says he, "you know that bad people congregate there, and you may be tempted." But she replies, "Never mind; if I sin I will repent of it afterwards."

You young people who are truly Christians are careful about spending too much time with inappropriate company. You are on your guard, for you are afraid you may be ensnared into sin. If you know what it is to be wounded by the arrows of sin in your soul, you will walk into apparent danger with caution and much prayer. You will surely be much on your guard. But if you say, "Oh, if I sin I will repent afterward," what must I say of you? You will repent, will you? And will this make everything right again so easily? Suppose you foresaw that, during a week's vacation, you would get drunk a few times and would commit one or two murders. Would you say, "Oh, I may still be a good Christian despite this. I will be careful to repent of it after it is all over"? Horrible! And yet you still think yourself a good Christian!

Let me tell you, a Christian man who repents of sin repents of it as sin. He does not distinguish between a little secret sin and a great sin like murder. He knows that there is no such distinction between sins; he cannot commit one without a second thought and then shrink from the other. With him, anything that grieves God is a horrible thing. With anything that displeases God, he cries out, "God will see it; it will grieve His heart!" His primary concern is always, How will this affect God? One who knows what it is to be guilty of sin before God, and then who knows also what it is to be delivered from this condition, will understand how the Christian feels in circumstances of temptation, where he is in danger of sinning. All his hair stands on end! How awful to sin against God! Therefore, anything that seems likely to bring him into danger will rouse up all his soul within him, and put him on his guard.

The unbelief of the church as to what believers may receive from Christ is the great stumbling block, hindering themselves and others from experiencing deliverance. Not only is this a great curse to professing Christians, but it is also a great grief and trial to Jesus Christ.

Many people seem to have hardened their hearts against all expectation of being delivered from sin. They have heard the doctrine preached. They have seen some people claim to be in this state of salvation from sin, but they have also seen some of these people fall again, and now they deliberately reject the whole doctrine. But is this consistent with really embracing the Gospel? What is Christ to the believer? What was His mission in the world? What is He doing, and what is He trying to do?

Christ has come to break the power of sin in the heart, and to be the life of the believer. He has come to work in him a perpetual salvation from sin, aiming to bring him in this way, and only this way, to heaven at last. What is faith if it is not the actual giving of yourself to Christ so that He may do this work for you and in you? What are you to believe of Christ if not this, that He is to save His people from their sins? (See Matthew 1:21.) Does the Bible tell you to expect something less than this? The fact is, the common experience of nominal Christians has misrepresented the truth. Those who have formed their views more from this experience than from the Bible have adopted exceedingly defective opinions about the nature and intent of the Gospel. They seem to forget altogether that Paul assured them that if they are under grace, sin will not have dominion over them (Rom. 6:14). When Christians do not expect this blessing from Christ, they will not get it.

One thing more must be said: there is a danger that many of the professing Christians of our day seem not to realize. The danger lies in having so much light concerning the provisions made in the Gospel for present sanctification, and then in rejecting this light and going on in sin as if the Gospel made no provision to save the Christian from his sins. How many rush blindly into this awful peril and to their own destruction!

I urge you to expect what God has promised in His Word. Paul said to the Romans, *"Reckon yourselves to be dead indeed to sin, but alive to God in Christ Jesus our Lord."* You may take these words for yourself this very day; entire deliverance from sin can be yours. According to your faith, you may expect to receive (Matt. 9:29).